The National Security Legacy of Harry S. Truman

The National Security Legacy of Harry S. Truman
Truman Legacy Series, Volume 1

Based on the First Truman Legacy Symposium
Harry Truman and National Security
June 13–14, 2003
Key West, Florida

Edited by
Robert P. Watson
Michael J. Devine
Robert J. Wolz

THE NATIONAL SECURITY LEGACY of HARRY S. TRUMAN

Edited By

Robert P. Watson
Michael J. Devine
Robert J. Wolz

Volume 1
Truman State University Press

Cover art: President Truman takes the presidential salute during a flag ceremony in Berlin, 21 July 1945. Photo by U.S. Navy, courtesy TPL, 63-1455-47.
Cover design: Shaun Hoffeditz
Type: Garamond Light, ITC Garamond is a registered trademark of International Typeface Corporation; Bauer Text Initials, copyright Phil's Fonts.
Printed by: McNaughton & Gunn, Inc., Saline, Michigan USA

Library of Congress Cataloging-in-Publication Data
Truman Legacy Symposium (1st : 2003 : Key West, Fla.)
   The national security legacy of Harry S. Truman / edited by Robert P. Watson, Michael J. Devine, Robert J. Wolz ; with forewords by Clifton Truman Daniel and Frank T. Brogan.
      p. cm. — (Truman legacy series; v. 1)
   Papers originally presented at first Truman Legacy Symposium: Harry Truman and National Security, June 13-14, 2003, held in Key West, Fla.
   Includes bibliographical references and index.
   ISBN 1-931112-46-0 (alk. paper)
1. Truman, Harry S., 1884-1972—Influence—Congresses. 2. Truman, Harry S., 1884-1972—Political and social views—Congresses. 3. United States—Foreign relations—1945-1953—Congresses. 4. National security—United States—History—20th century—Congresses. 5. Cold War—Congresses. 6. Presidents—United States—Congresses. I. Watson, Robert P., 1962- II. Devine, Michael J., 1945- III. Wolz, Robert J. IV. Title. V. Series.
   E814.T85 2005
   355'.033073'09044—dc22

                                                              2004024691

CONTENTS

LIFE OF HARRY S. TRUMAN

WORKING FOR TRUMAN

TRUMAN & NATIONAL SECURITY

Photographs

TPL . . . . *Harry S. Truman Presidential Museum and Library*
LWH. . . . . *Harry S. Truman Little White House Museum*

Foreword

One of the things about being Harry Truman's grandson is that wherever I go, people ask me to talk about him. I'm honored to do that, but I'm no expert on Harry Truman. He did not get many chances to impart political and historical wisdom to me. I had only been alive for fifteen years when he died, and he'd had to spend much of that time telling me to keep my feet off the tables and quit running in the house. As a result, much of what I know about his career comes from reading and listening to experts, people who worked with him and for him. In that regard, I've been very lucky, because my grandfather surrounded himself with some of the smartest, most dedicated people in government.

George Elsey, Ken Hechler, and Milton Kayle, who have contributed to this book, served the Truman administration honorably and effectively. All went on from the White House to distinguished careers—Milt as a prominent attorney, George as head of the American Red Cross and the White House Historical Association, and Ken as a congressman and secretary of state of West Virginia. (At nearly ninety-one, he was a percentage point away from being elected again!) Joining them in the following pages is General Brent Scowcroft, national security advisor to two presidents, who is able to put into perspective the effect my grandfather's mid-twentieth-century policies have had on U.S. foreign policy and national security to this day.

My grandfather was famous for saying that there was nothing new in the world but the history you don't know, and I think that philosophy was one of the things that made him a great president. He knew very well the mistakes that leaders and nations had made over millennia, and he knew history would only repeat itself if he didn't do things differently. In doing just that, he reshaped the world for the better.

Clifton Truman Daniel
June 2003

Foreword

Many great people contributed to the unique Truman Legacy Symposium upon which this book is based. I say unique because it is rare that one has the opportunity to hear about the history of our world from such eminent scholars as those who contributed to this book, but it is even more rare that one gets to hear about history from people who were there to shape it.

Legacy is an interesting word. Too many people in elected positions try to plan their legacies. This is a serious mistake because legacies are not decided upon by those who leave them, but are determined more often than not by circumstances during one's tenure in office. And what a person leaves behind is not considered a legacy until it has been tested by the passage of time and by the careful consideration of its consequences by those who follow.

I believe the legacy of Harry Truman speaks for itself. In this book, you will read a great deal about it from those who lived through Truman's presidency and helped shape it, and from those who are studying it, many of whom were not even born until decades after his presidency ended. But assessing legacies is an evolutionary process; scholars will be constantly working at it and it will continue unfolding for generations to come. Harry Truman's legacy is becoming greater with each passing year largely because he made his decisions by surrounding himself with great people and then trying to do what all great leaders should do at the end of the day—the right thing. And he did so without thought to what those decisions might mean generations later in terms of legacy. By listening to his advisors and by making each decision according to what he believed was right, he was able ultimately to know that "the buck stopped here"—with him. The right decision needed to be made at the right time. And I think that is part of the true genius of Truman.

I suspect my connection to Harry Truman is that we shared something in common in public life. I had the pleasure to serve for five years as Florida's lieutenant governor, and Truman served his country as Franklin D. Roosevelt's vice president before becoming president. There is a story about lieutenant governors and vice presidents, both of whom often find themselves awash in a sea of anonymity: A woman gave birth to twin sons, one of whom went off to sea, while the other became a lieutenant governor (or vice president). It seems that neither was ever heard from again!

But I have had the pleasure of becoming the president of Florida Atlantic University, which is honored to be an official sponsor of the Truman Legacy Symposium and this book. Both projects mark the first in a series of efforts to assess Truman's legacy and his connection to south Florida and the Little White House in the Florida Keys, a home where Truman spent 175 days during his presidency. Florida Atlantic University is pleased to have helped to bring together people of such great historical significance as George Elsey, Ken Hechler, and Milton Kayle, all of whom worked for President Harry Truman. The symposium organizers and editors of this volume—Robert Watson, Michael Devine, and Bob Wolz—have brought together a wonderful group of men and women to assess Truman's legacy. It gives me great pleasure to introduce this book and these individuals.

"Give 'em hell, Harry!"

Frank T. Brogan, President,
Florida Atlantic University
June 2003

Preface

Harry S. Truman called Key West, Florida, his second favorite place—second only to his hometown of Independence, Missouri. In fact, Truman was so fond of Key West that he ended up spending a total of 175 days of his presidency at the "Little White House," as his presidential retreat came to be known. The president even joked that he was of a mind "to move the Capitol to Key West." The thirty-third president made eleven trips to Key West during his presidency to escape the pressures of office and the nation's capital. But the Little White House and tropical allure of Key West proved to be more than a relaxing vacation site or Truman's version of Camp David; rather, the facility was a working White House. Truman studied legislation, signed executive orders, and met with politicians and advisors during his time on "America's Caribbean Island." Truman and his family even returned to Key West several times after his presidency.

So it is fitting that the historic occasion of the fiftieth anniversary of the end of Truman's presidency was celebrated in Key West with public and scholarly programs dedicated to examining Truman's presidential legacy. This book is an outgrowth of the Truman Legacy Symposium, which was held on 13–14 June 2003 in Key West, Florida. The purpose of this symposium, the first in a series, was to assess Truman's national security legacy. Each symposium and its accompanying book will focus on a different facet of Truman's legacy, and perhaps no other issue was as timely on the date of the first symposium as national security. Likewise, although the Truman presidential record is as impressively wide as it is deep, no other issue has stood out over the years in defining Harry Truman's legacy so much as national security.

Historians credit Truman with establishing the twin policies of containment and collective security, approaches to national security that defined U.S. foreign policy for a half century. In a larger sense, from the rise of the Cold War to the collapse of the Soviet Union, these twin pillars guided the international order and the

West's response to communist threats and international instability. Harry Truman presided over the creation of the United Nations and the North Atlantic Treaty Organization (NATO), the organization of a unified Department of Defense, the modern Air Force, the Central Intelligence Agency (CIA), and National Security Council (NSC), and the use of foreign aid and food aid as major tools in promoting stability, democracy, and U.S. foreign policy— a formidable record indeed. As Truman, himself a dedicated student of history, suggested:

> When history says that my term of office saw the beginning of the Cold War it will also say that in those eight years we have set the course that can win it. We have succeeded in carving out a new set of policies to attain peace—positive policies, policies of world leadership, policies that express faith in other free people. We have averted World War III up to now, and we may already have succeeded in establishing conditions which can keep that war from happening as far ahead as men can see.

Still, it must be remembered that Harry Truman's accomplishments were not immediately apparent to his contemporaries. The tough decisions we now praise Truman for making also made him, at times, an unpopular president. Since presidential approval polls have been taken, Truman has the distinction of having the lowest recorded rating (in the 20s), even lower than Richard Nixon on the eve of his resignation from the office. But the years have been good to Truman, as his stature among presidents and his image among the public have improved considerably.

When thinking of pivotal figures from the past, many students of history are tempted to speculate about what these voices from yesteryear would say about today's issues. It is also irresistible to ponder what they would say to these larger-than-life leaders from history. As historians and Truman aficionados, we often find ourselves thinking about Truman in this light. Our hypothetical conversation with Truman goes this way: we would tell him to make sure he is seated because he is not going to believe that he is now universally admired! More presidential candidates—of both parties—in recent elections have cited Truman as their role model than any other president. In evaluating Truman and his legacy, historians now judge him to have been one of the great presidents.

Truman had great faith in the American people (even when they opposed him) and an almost uncanny ability (and foresight) to be on the right side of the issues, however challenging and controversial they were. These qualities must certainly be a part of his legacy. Part of the process of assessing presidential legacies is to assess the impact of the office on the man. In many ways, the man who entered the office in 1945 was the same man who stepped down from power in 1953. Truman was always humble, hard working, and honest. This humility can be seen in his surprise after leaving office at finding a crowd of five thousand people gathered to welcome him home to the Trumans' house on Delaware Street in Independence. In typical fashion, Truman admitted, "I was overcome." But also in typical fashion, Truman added, "It was the pay-off for 30 years of hell and hard work."

Another facet in the process of determining a president's legacy is to judge the impact of the president's service. Did he leave the office and nation better off than when he entered the White House? In contemplating legacies, Truman once remarked, "The best epitaph I ever saw was on Butte Hill in Tombstone, Arizona. It said 'Here lies Jack Williams. He done His damndest'." It must be said that Harry Truman did his damnedest, and both the office and nation are better off because of him.

As the conveners of the Truman Legacy Symposium and editors of this book, our effort to examine Truman's legacy was greatly enhanced by three distinguished gentlemen who were with Truman in the White House (and in Key West). George Elsey, Ken Hechler, and Milton Kayle, all former aides to President Truman who went on to remarkably successful post-White House public careers, lent their formidable talents and personal experiences to the task of assessing Truman's record and Truman the man. It is easier to understand the extraordinary accomplishments of the Truman administration once one is afforded the opportunity to appreciate the abilities and dedication of those Truman chose to surround himself with. This project also benefits immeasurably by the participation of General Brent Scowcroft, national security advisor to two presidents and one of the foremost national security experts of our time. We were also fortunate to include the work of four very well-regarded scholars of the presidency and national security: Meena Bose of the U.S. Military Academy, Douglas Brattebo of the U.S. Naval Academy, John Davis of Howard University, and Tom Lansford of the University of Southern Mississippi.

We also wish to thank the hosts of the inaugural symposium, without whom neither that event nor this book would have been possible: the Harry S. Truman Little White House, the Truman Presidential Museum and Library, the Florida Keys Community College, and Florida Atlantic University. Many individuals are to be credited with helping to make both endeavors a reality. It is not possible to name everyone but, in particular, we acknowledge Wanda Coury, former clerk and secretary in the Truman White House; Niel Johnson, noted Truman impersonator; Kathy Knotts and Donna Denslow of the Harry S. Truman Library Institute; Barbara Hayo and Monica Muñoz of Historic Tours of America; Lydia Esteñoz, Michael McPherson, and William Seeker of the Florida Keys Community College; Rebecca Tomlinson of the Tennessee Williams Theater; Mary Dean, Richard Yon, David Cantor, and Shawn Pennell of Florida Atlantic University; Raymond Frey; Wesley Truman Daniel; and Debra Corona of Simple Office Solutions. A special thanks to the Crowne Plaza La Concha Hotel in Key West for accommodating the symposium participants and guests, to Key West's popular Conch Train for providing transportation for symposium participants and guests, and to the Truman State University Press for their enthusiastic reception of this book project.

Four individuals threw their support behind our vision for an annual symposium and book series to assess Truman's legacy and, in doing so, made our task much easier. To Ed Swift, President, and Chris Belland, CEO, of Historic Tours of America; to Frank T. Brogan, President of Florida Atlantic University; and to Clifton Truman Daniel, grandson of President Truman—thank you for your commitment to historic preservation, community educational programs, and Harry Truman's memory. Lastly, a number of individuals and organizations underwrote the symposium and, indirectly, this book. We are grateful for the generosity of Charna Larkin and the Alan B. Larkin Family, the John D. Evans Foundation, Historic Tours of America, the Harry S. Truman Library Institute, the Key West Harry Truman Foundation, and the Monroe County Tourist Development Council.

We hope you find the book to be informative and interesting.

Robert P. Watson, Florida Atlantic
University, Boca Raton, Florida
Michael J. Devine, Truman Presidential
Library, Independence, Missouri
Robert J. Wolz, Harry S. Truman Little
White House, Key West, Florida
June 2003

LIFE OF
HARRY S.
TRUMAN

THE MAN FROM MISSOURI

Robert P. Watson

EARLY YEARS

Harry S. Truman was born on 8 May 1884 in Lamar, Missouri. The firstborn child of John Anderson Truman and Martha Ellen (Young), Truman was named for his uncle, Harrison Young. Because Harry Truman's parents diplomatically selected the middle initial S for their son in place of a middle name, both Solomon Young, the maternal grandfather, and Anderson Ship Truman, the paternal grandfather, could also claim the boy as a namesake. Two more children—a boy, Vivian, and a girl, Mary Jane—would be born to John and Martha Truman.

The Truman family was of modest means and struggled to make ends meet by working the land in rural Missouri. As a result, the family frequently moved in search of better economic opportunities. The first move occurred in 1887 when the Trumans took up residence at a farm near Grandview, Missouri. In 1890 they moved to Independence; in 1902, after John Truman lost a considerable amount of money in grain speculation, the family was again forced to move, this time to Kansas City.

Harry Truman was a bright child and developed a love for reading at an early age, especially enjoying the topic of history. His mother, with whom Harry enjoyed a loving relationship, encouraged his aptitude for the piano by enrolling him in lessons in Kansas City; Truman would grow to be an accomplished pianist. Truman attended public schools, graduating in 1901 from the high school in Independence, but he did not graduate near the top of his class and was, overall, an unremarkable student. Hindered by poor eyesight and obliged to help with the family farm, Harry's participation in extracurricular activities was limited. The

Trumans could not afford the costs of college so, after graduating from high school, Truman worked as a timekeeper for a railroad construction project, then as a clerk for two different banks in Kansas City. His father's poor health prevented Truman from pursuing a career in banking or setting out on his own in Kansas City. In 1906, the eldest son moved with the family back to Grandview to work the farm owned by his maternal grandmother.

In total, Truman devoted over a decade of his life to farming. Noted Truman biographer Robert Ferrell says of Truman's main occupation:

> Truman's preparation for the presidency began with his early life on the farm, the kind of experience that many a lad in the years before and just after the twentieth century never forgot.... After 1950 it no longer was important for politicians to boast that they had been born and raised on a farm.[1]

Indeed, Truman was no stranger to hard work; throughout his political career, his legendary ability to connect to, as well as his lifelong commitment to serve, ordinary people stemmed from his humble upbringing. Because his story mirrored that of so many of his countrymen at the time, Truman would come to embody the consummate American underdog.

MILITARY SERVICE AND MARRIAGE

In 1905, Truman enlisted in the Missouri National Guard, where he served until 1911. With the outbreak of war in Europe a few years later, Truman quickly reenlisted and helped to organize the 2nd Regiment of the Missouri Field Artillery. World War I was the defining event of the time, but it was a major event in Truman's life for other reasons. Truman had never before traveled farther outside his native state than Kansas City, Kansas. When his unit was called into service as part of the 129th Field Artillery in the European theater, Truman saw action on several battlefields in France, including Meuse-Argonne, Saint Mihiel, and Vosges.

During the war, the former Missouri farmer was promoted to the rank of captain and was placed in command of Battery D of the artillery regiment. Truman earned the respect of his men for his bravery under fire and ability to assert his authority when the entire battery began to flee in disarray in the face of enemy fire.

Harry S.
Truman in
World War I
uniform, 1917.
(TPL, 79-18)

Both the war and his feats of courage instilled in Truman a sense of confidence and caught the attention of neighbors back home. Truman ultimately rose to the rank of colonel; many years later when America began preparing for World War II, he again attempted to reenlist. (He was serving as a U.S. senator at the time.) However, his request was denied by Army Chief of Staff General George C. Marshall.

The years before and during World War I were significant for Truman in another way. By the outbreak of the war, Truman was seriously courting Elizabeth "Bess" Wallace. Harry Truman's life-long interest in Bess began when the Trumans moved to Independence in 1890 and five-year-old Bess and six-year-old Harry attended the same Sunday school. Even though he had long sought her hand in marriage, the couple's wedding plans were put on hold by a cautious Truman, who wanted to wait until after the war to spare his fiancée the possibility of being widowed or married to a soldier maimed by the horrors of war. They were eventually married on 28 June 1919. A daughter, Mary Margaret, was born on 17 February 1924. Harry Truman's deep devotion to Bess lasted until his death.[2]

POLITICS

Truman returned from the war to establish Truman & Jacobson, a men's clothing store he ran with his friend from the war, Eddie Jacobson. However, their Kansas City haberdashery failed and left the two partners bankrupt and facing considerable debt. After several years and much effort, Truman managed to repay the roughly $35,000 he owed. Business was not Truman's calling.

The dominant force in Missouri politics in the 1920s was the Pendergast family. Jim Pendergast, the patriarch, had served as an alderman in Kansas City for almost twenty years, during which time he exerted influence over who was elected and what local politicians did. After Jim's death in 1911, his brother, Tom, took over the political machine. The Pendergast machine continued to influence the nomination and election of public officials and doled out jobs in return for loyalty at the polls to the Pendergast slate of candidates. Tom Pendergast delivered a lot of votes for his candidates, including a political novice named Harry Truman. Historian Richard Lawrence Miller described Pendergast's influence: "At one polling place [Truman] watched men going round and round in a circle, casting one ballot after another." Award-winning Truman biographer David McCullough noted that the Pendergasts were good at assuring that voters "voted early and often" on election day.[3]

Truman came to the attention of Tom Pendergast through his friendship with Pendergast's nephew, Jim. Truman's first foray into politics came in 1922 when he won the opportunity to serve on the three-judge Jackson County Court in Missouri. The position was not a true judgeship but rather functioned much as a county administrator. Truman was defeated in his bid for reelection in 1924—the only election he would ever lose—but was successful in regaining the office in 1926.

It is ironic that Harry Truman cut his political teeth as part of Tom Pendergast's network because by 1934 Truman had emerged as a New Dealer and honest political reformer, commitments he would carry with him throughout his long political career. With a reputation as an honest, hardworking man who remembered the people and got things done, Truman was asked by Pendergast to run for a seat in the U.S. Senate in 1934. Truman needed Pendergast's help to win a statewide race and Pendergast recognized in Truman a Democratic Party loyalist and hard worker. Truman had, after all, made sure the roads were paved. With Pendergast's support, Truman was elected to the Senate.

Truman would eventually serve in the Senate with great distinction, although his first term was marked by neither notoriety nor remarkable legislative accomplishment. Moreover, Truman came to the august body marred by his ties to Pendergast and lacking a college education; as such, he was not highly regarded by his colleagues. Truman always remained friends with Tom Pendergast, even after his former benefactor was convicted of income tax evasion in 1939, a fact which says more about Truman's sense of responsibility than it does about Pendergast's influence on Truman's political record. Truman tempered his loyalty to Pendergast with his own moral compass.

That first term in the Senate saw Truman emerge as a key proponent of the Civil Aeronautics Act of 1938 and cosponsor of the Transportation Act of 1940, known as the Wheeler-Truman Act (for Senator Burton Wheeler of Montana). Truman also championed labor unions and was both a loyal Democrat and an advocate of President Roosevelt's New Deal social programs. Yet the president did not reward the Missouri senator for his loyalty;

Senator Truman at Truman Committee hearing to investigate the National Defense Program, ca. 1943. From left to right: Senator James Mead, Charles Patrick Clark, Jesse Jones, Senator Harry S. Truman, Senator Ralph O. Brewster, Senator Joseph Ball, Senator Gerald Nye. (TPL, 58-442)

it would not be until his second term that Truman gained the nation's attention.

After being reelected in 1940, the highlight of Truman's second term was his service as chairman of the Senate's Special Committee to Investigate the National Defense Program. In 1941, the committee commenced the important work of making sure the Department of War and its contractors were acting efficiently and in good faith in the procurement and production of military equipment and supplies necessary for the war effort. Truman took bold positions and was undeterred by the powerful forces arrayed against him. His committee uncovered and reined in abuses by defense contractors, ensured fair prices for military goods, improved poor workmanship, and worked to prevent shortages of precious minerals and other materials. The work of the Truman Committee, as it came to be known, aided FDR's lend-lease program (supplying Great Britain with supplies and weapons) and, later, the war effort. Truman held over four hundred hearings, issued a total of fifty reports, and visited numerous military bases and defense production facilities. For his role as head of the committee, Truman gained national attention.

By 1944, the Democratic Party was in turmoil despite its popular, long-serving leader, Franklin Roosevelt. FDR had managed to masterfully weave together an unlikely assortment of southern Democrats, progressive northern liberals, union members, blacks, and others, but it was becoming increasingly difficult to hold the patchwork together, a situation that would only be exacerbated in the postwar era. Indeed, important questions loomed regarding the ending of the war and how to deal with the domestic agenda and economy once hostilities ceased. It was also apparent to some that FDR's health was slipping and the party would soon need a new standard-bearer. A number of individuals emerged as likely vice presidential candidates for the 1944 ticket, but most were unacceptable to one faction of the party or another.

It was into this sensitive situation that Harry Truman was thrust. A reluctant vice presidential candidate, Truman neither desired nor sought the office but accepted it only after a direct, personal appeal from the president. Truman was nominated as the Democratic vice presidential candidate at the Chicago convention in July 1944. The Roosevelt-Truman ticket would go on to defeat Thomas E. Dewey and John W. Bricker, giving FDR an unprecedented fourth term in the White House. Truman was sworn in on

20 January 1945. Only eighty-three days later, President Roosevelt died while vacationing in Warm Springs, Georgia. Truman became the nation's thirty-third president on 12 April 1945.

THE PRESIDENCY

Crafting a New International Order

If ever a new president was thrust into a challenge, that president was Harry Truman. It is always a sensitive and difficult matter for a president to assume the office on the death of his predecessor, but it was especially so for Truman, given both the monumental events of the time and the fact that FDR had been the longest-serving president in history and the beloved leader who shepherded the nation through the Great Depression and World War II. Yet Truman literally shaped history within the first few months of his presidency. The war in Europe was ending, and important decisions had to be made about the postwar era and about the conduct of the conflict in the Pacific theater.

Truman's first two months in office saw the suicide of Adolph Hitler and the unconditional surrender of Nazi Germany. Truman presided over the important conference at Potsdam in Germany that established the framework for postwar Germany and, to a degree, postwar Europe. While shaping policy in Europe, Truman still had to contend with continued Japanese hostilities in the Pacific theater. Although Japan's end was apparent, many Japanese leaders were unwilling to surrender, and the United States faced the prospect of rooting Japanese forces from their defensive positions island by island and the possibility of invading Japan. All scenarios for the invasion predicted that Japan would fight to the last man in a protracted and costly campaign. The Battle of Okinawa, after all, had been one of the bloodiest of the war, with roughly 48,000 American and 100,000 Japanese casualties.

The Manhattan Project was begun in secret in 1939 at the Los Alamos laboratory in New Mexico under the direction of physicist Robert Oppenheimer. By July 1945, the project had produced and successfully tested an atomic bomb, offering a new option to bring about a quicker, less costly end to the war. However, upon entering office, Truman had been largely unaware of the details of the bomb. In a matter of weeks, he was forced to assess this new lethal weapon in the U.S. arsenal. Truman had sought an

President Truman delivering his inaugural address, 20 January 1949.
(U.S. Army/courtesy TPL, 64-1-55)

unconditional surrender from imperial Japan but was rebuffed, and therefore on 25 July approved the potential deployment of the A-bomb. The following day, the United States, joined by Great Britain and China, again asked Japan to surrender. Again they were rebuffed. In Truman's words:

> It was to spare the Japanese people from utter destruction that the ultimatum of July 26 was issued at Potsdam. Their leaders promptly rejected that ultimatum. If they do not now accept our terms they may expect a rain of ruin from the air, the like of which has never been seen on this earth.[4]

Truman ordered the first bomb to be dropped 6 August 1945 on Hiroshima. Even though the bomb killed 75,000 Japanese

instantly and resulted in countless additional radiation-related ill-
nesses and deaths, Japan again refused to surrender. A second
bomb was dropped on 9 August on the city of Nagasaki, killing
another 75,000 people. Emperor Hirohito authorized the surrender of Japan on 14 August 1945, and Truman permitted him to
remain symbolically on his throne. Although the dropping of the
bombs remains a controversial issue, it hastened the end of the
war and saved tens of thousands of lives on both sides.

Even with the war ended, Truman had little time to savor the
victory, as a number of other pressing international concerns
remained. Europe was devastated, America was poised for the
first time in its history to assume the role of world leader, and the
tensions with the Soviet Union began to deteriorate further. The
USSR soon emerged as a new enemy to international peace. The
expansionist campaign of the Soviets resulted in Communist rule
in Albania, Bulgaria, Hungary, Poland, Romania, and Yugoslavia,
all by 1947, with the very real prospect of further Soviet aggression. A new, "cold" war faced the allies as articulated by George
Kennan, a diplomat in the U.S. embassy in Moscow, who is often
credited with delivering one of the first public warnings of the
Soviet's aggressive imperial intentions.[5] Winston Churchill echoed
these sentiments by eloquently describing an "iron curtain" falling
across Europe, dividing East and West ideologically. After initially
attempting to maintain a relationship with the Soviet Union, Truman and his staff took the warnings of Churchill and Kennan to
heart and crafted a policy to contain Soviet influence and unite
the western world.

Truman's postwar leadership in the face of Soviet threats
shaped international affairs for at least a half century. Indeed, in
his first year alone, Truman ushered in a new approach to American foreign policy, positioned the United States as world leader,
and planted the seeds for a new international relationship built
around collective security; in so doing, he established himself as
one of the most important and active presidents in the areas of
international affairs and national security.[6]

The Truman Doctrine

In meeting the threat of the new postwar world, Truman organized what was to become the framework for American national
security by establishing such institutions as the Central Intelligence Agency and the National Security Agency and creating a

unified Department of Defense. His approach to preventing the expansion of the Soviets and Communism involved maintaining the nation's firm resolve to oppose Communism at all costs and to provide U.S. military and economic aid to countries fighting or threatened by communist insurgency—a policy that became known as the Truman Doctrine. The doctrine was initially developed to address the civil war in Greece and the Soviet threat to Turkey. Truman appealed to Congress for U.S. aid for Greece and Turkey; the $400 million aid package helped to forego communist expansion. Truman debuted the new doctrine in a speech to Congress on 12 March 1947:

> I believe that it must be the policy of the United States to support free peoples who are resisting attempted subjugation by armed minorities or by outside pressures. I believe that we must assist free peoples to work out their own destinies in their own way. I believe that our help should be primarily through economic and financial aid which is essential to economic stability and orderly political processes.[7]

The Marshall Plan and the Berlin Airlift

Truman was successful in Greece and Turkey, but more was needed. Europe was still plagued by economic crises, reduced industrial and agricultural production, hyperinflation, trade imbalances, and political instability. The United States had provided roughly $9 billion in aid to Europe during the war, but Truman realized further U.S. action was necessary to stabilize the Continent. In 1947, U.S. delegates met with key European allies in Paris to discuss the reconstruction of Europe, and Truman appointed his trusted ally, General George Marshall, to develop a program for reconstructing Europe. Marshall publicly unveiled the proposal on 5 June 1947 during a commencement address at Harvard University, where he stated:

> The truth of the matter is that Europe's requirements for the next three or four years of foreign food and other essential products—principally from America—are so much greater than her present ability to pay that she must have substantial additional help or face economic, social, and political deterioration of a very grave character.... It is logical that the United States should do whatever it is able to do to assist in the return of normal economic health in the world, without which there can be no political stability and no assured peace.[8]

Truman's proposal was successful, as Congress generously funded the Economic Cooperation Act in 1948. The United States provided nearly $14 billion in aid from 1948 through 1951, including food, agricultural equipment, fuel, machinery, and an assortment of other vital goods and services to the war-torn region, thereby securing Europe's future as a stable ally of the United States. The European recovery program became known for its author, George Marshall, and the Truman administration was again credited with preventing political upheaval and stemming the influence of Communism. For his efforts, Marshall was awarded the Nobel Peace Prize in 1953.

Another international security crisis arose in 1948, this time dividing the East and West quite literally. The Soviet Union, then in control of East Germany and Eastern Europe, declared that the allies had no authority in the former German capital of Berlin. The Soviet blockade of Berlin cut off all access to the city; the flow of essential goods and services ended, and Berliners were threatened with starvation. A full-scale confrontation loomed between the Soviets and the West. Truman wisely resisted the use of force and responded with a plan reflecting both the Truman Doctrine and the Marshall Plan. In June 1948, the United States commenced an unprecedented airlift that brought tons of food, fuel, and other products to the isolated population. The airlift lasted until September 1949, when the Soviets lifted their blockade of the city.

The United Nations and NATO

As a new president, Harry Truman had the historic opportunity in July 1945 to sign the charter establishing the United Nations. Truman also presided over the creation of the North Atlantic Treaty Organization (NATO), a military alliance designed to oppose the Soviets and unite Western Europe with the United States in a grand effort to promote collective security. Under the terms of the treaty, an attack on one NATO member was considered an attack on all NATO members. At its founding in 1949, NATO included the United States, Belgium, Canada, Denmark, France, Great Britain, Iceland, Italy, Luxembourg, the Netherlands, Norway, and Portugal. These organizations that Truman helped to create and promote have remained a central part of U.S. foreign policy and international security for the half century since his presidency.

The Korean War

In 1948, Korea had split into two nations after Communists took over the northern part of the country. On 25 June 1950, North Korea invaded South Korea, and the forces of the Democratic People's Republic of Korea teetered on the brink of collapse. Although Truman was working to reduce military spending, he was forced to retool U.S. military capabilities in response to North Korea's invasion and military success. The consequences of the North's victory for the larger worldwide struggle against Communism were such that Truman ordered U.S. forces to aid South Korea in 1950. The Korean War was technically not a war in that neither Truman nor the U.S. Congress ever officially declared war; rather, Truman deemed it a police action and had international support for the U.S. deployment. It is said that the war ended in a draw, but the United States did prevent the North Koreans from controlling their neighbors to the south, recaptured the important capital city of Seoul, and drove the Communists out of South Korea, making the effort a success for the South Koreans and the Truman Doctrine.

Israel

Zionists had long sought to establish a Jewish nation and had planned, convened conferences, and sought international support for such a state in Palestine. As early as 1917, Great Britain had supported a Jewish homeland with the Balfour Declaration. By the late 1930s, Jews were being persecuted and killed by the Nazis, the future of Jews in parts of Europe and the Soviet Union looked bleak, and the British had their plate full with the fascist threat in Europe. The dream would have to wait until after World War II.

Almost 100,000 Holocaust survivors entered Palestine between 1945 and 1948, but the question of a Jewish state lingered. The UN and the international community worked unsuccessfully to solve the matter, and the UN handed the dilemma of separating Palestine into Arab and Jewish sections over to Great Britain. In a historic act on 14 May 1948, Jewish leaders established the state of Israel. Truman initially opposed the creation of a new state because he favored joint governance by Arabs and Jews, but he was certainly sympathetic to the plight of Jews in Palestine and Europe. Truman made the decision to support the partition, even though the bold action was unpopular among many of his aides. In 1948, Truman formally recognized the exist-ence and rights of Israel, making the United States the first nation to support Israel, an act that occasioned further international sup-port and helped to legitimize Jewish claims for nationhood.

The Fair Deal

Truman drafted the blueprint for the postwar international order—few presidents can claim such an extensive legacy on a global scale—yet, he was far from idle on the domestic front. He continued, and even expanded, the focus of his predecessor's New Deal programs by promoting a range of social and eco-nomic initiatives to strengthen the economy and expand oppor-tunities for all Americans. Truman's own social policies became known as the Fair Deal.

One of Truman's most difficult challenges was making the transition from a wartime economy to a peacetime economy. High levels of production for the defense effort were no longer needed in a time of peace, but demilitarizing without harming the economy, while absorbing the many veterans seeking employment, required careful attention. Truman was most sensi-tive to the need to create jobs that paid a fair wage. In his words, "the foundations of a healthy national economy cannot be secure so long as any large section of our working people receive sub-standard wages."[9]

Truman's vision for such a jobs program and the Fair Deal was spelled out in an address to Congress on 6 September 1945, where he called for increases in Social Security benefits, a higher minimum wage, basic wage and price controls, and even a national health insurance measure. He would ultimately be suc-cessful only on the first two items of this ambitious program. Also among his domestic accomplishments were a public housing bill and historic civil rights legislation. On many issues, however, the president encountered opposition from Republicans in Congress; the defeat of Truman's own party in the midterm elections of 1946 made the passage of the Fair Deal programs even more dif-ficult. Yet the president persisted and was reelected in 1948. The Democrats regained control of both houses of Congress, but lost many seats in the 1950 election.

Another challenge of the postwar economy was the relation-ship between labor and big business, which was increasingly being defined by fighting and threats of strikes. Truman waded right into the thick of several major strikes that threatened to undermine economic growth in the critical years immediately after the war, including the steel industry, General Motors, and the United Mine Workers. The notorious Taft-Hartley Act, sponsored by Senator Robert Taft (son of President William Howard Taft) and Representative Fred Hartley, empowered the federal government with an injunction directed at strikes believed to threaten national security. But the legislation also eliminated unions' ability to contribute to political campaigns, banned certain types of boycotts, and contained rabid anticommunist oaths and requirements for union employees and union membership. Truman disliked the legislation but wanted the power to intervene in strikes of economically vital industries.

Truman vetoed the bill in 1947 but was overridden by a Congress bent on responding to the strikes in any manner necessary and under pressure from knee-jerk anticommunists. Despite his opposition to the bill, Truman did intervene when he deemed it necessary. One such occasion involved his attempt to end a strike by steelworkers in 1952. Truman was concerned that the strike, occurring in the thick of the Korean War, would threaten national security, as the United States could not win the war without the factories that produced munitions and weapons. Accordingly, Truman called on the government to seize the mills, an action that produced immediate and loud criticism from across the nation, including even calls to impeach the president. Truman was ultimately unsuccessful, as the U.S. Supreme Court ruled six to three against his effort to seize the steel mills. Despite these problems, Truman did manage to shepherd the nation from a wartime to a peacetime economy, then back to a limited wartime economy.

Civil Rights

Perhaps most notable among Truman's domestic victories were his civil rights initiatives, which included creating the first civil rights commission, desegregating the armed forces, and making discrimination by federal contractors illegal. Throughout his presidency, Truman prodded his Justice Department attorneys to defend plaintiffs fighting against segregation. It must be noted that Truman supported civil rights over the advice of many senior aides and at a time in history when white support for both civil rights and the president was weak. This not only demonstrated great personal and political courage, but also reflected Truman's personal maturation as one able to overcome his upbringing in rural Missouri, a family ancestry that included slave owners, and the beliefs of his own adored mother, who was an unapologetic segregationist. In the words of historian Richard Lawrence Miller, "Truman's prejudice makes his civil rights record all the more remarkable. ...This shows not only a genuine tolerance for others but a firm belief in the idea of America as a land of opportunity."[10]

Indeed, Truman promoted civil rights at great political cost to himself. In 1946, after losing both houses of Congress, Truman created a presidential committee on civil rights; he also supported a report by leading clergy and reformers that called for efforts to combat discrimination. The decision to integrate the armed forces was made in 1948, a presidential election year, amidst an uphill struggle against New York governor Thomas Dewey. This action invited criticism from his own military commanders and opened Truman to opposition from his southern Democratic base. Southern "Dixiecrat" Strom Thurmond decided to enter the presidential race on a segregationist, states' rights platform largely in response to Truman's initiatives. In his message to Congress on 2 February 1948 on the need for antilynching laws, fair employment practices, and other civil rights measures, Truman stated:

> This nation was founded by men and women who sought these shores that they might enjoy greater freedom and greater opportunities than they had known before. The founders of the United States proclaimed to the world the American belief that all men are created equal, and that governments are instituted to secure the inalienable rights with which all men are endowed.... The Federal Government has a clear duty to see that constitutional guarantees of individual liberties and of equal protection under the laws are not denied or abridged anywhere in our Union. That duty is shared by all three branches of the Government, but it can be fulfilled only if the Congress enacts modern, comprehensive civil rights laws.[11]

President Truman was unable to get much of what he wanted due to opposition from Republicans and southern Democrats in Congress. But Truman was undeterred and overcame the legislative failure by instead utilizing presidential executive orders, such as E.O. 9981, which mandated the integration of the armed forces.

AFTER THE PRESIDENCY

The image of Truman emblazoned in the minds of most Americans is of the president grinning as he displays the mistaken headline of the *Chicago Daily Tribune* newspaper proclaiming "Dewey Defeats Truman." Truman won reelection in that famous 1948 race, marking one of the biggest upsets in presidential history. Another popular image of Truman captured in newsreels of the day, romanticized in textbooks on government and politics, and extolled by present-day politicians is his famous whistle-stop train campaign tour. In a way, both images are fitting insofar as Truman was always the underdog and he was always one to both take his case directly to the people and keep their best interests at the forefront of his political ideology.

As appropriate as these images are, there is so much more to Truman's legacy. The president did not seek reelection in 1952,

Truman talks with high school students in Independence, Missouri, 8 May 1970. (TPL, 70-6130)

announcing the decision to retire on 29 March 1952. Yet, he had long before made up his mind to leave public office of his own accord, much as the figures from history he so admired, Cincinnatus and George Washington, had done. He informed key aides of his intention: "I know I could not be reelected again and continue to break the old precedent that was broken by FDR. It should not be done. That precedent should continue…by custom based on the honor of the man in the office."[12]

Truman retired from public life in January of 1953 and returned to his hometown of Independence to a warm welcome. Having spent close to three decades in public life and office— including many years away from home in Washington—Truman took to calling himself "Mr. Citizen" in retirement.[13] As an ex-president, Truman devoted considerable time to his passions of reading and writing. He also continued taking his brisk walks, lectured publicly, traveled to Europe with Bess, and invested a lot of energy into the building of the Truman Presidential Library, which he dedicated in 1957.

Harry Truman's health deteriorated in the 1960s, especially after he suffered a bad fall in the bathroom in 1964. On 5 December 1972, he was admitted to a hospital in Kansas City with symptoms of fatigue and lung congestion. Over the ensuing three weeks the former president weakened considerably and never recovered. On Christmas Day, he was in a coma; the thirty-third president died on 26 December 1972. Bess Truman survived her husband for almost another decade, passing away on 18 October 1982.

An unlikely hero, Truman overcame his humble beginnings, poor eyesight, the lack of a college education, and business failures to rise to the country's highest office, in which he shaped the postwar world both at home and abroad. In his first turbulent year as president, Truman set a course that ultimately won peace in post–World War II Europe and, much later, the Cold War. He aptly and humbly referred to his first year in office as a "year of decisions."[14] Not seen as especially charismatic or gifted politically, Truman was nonetheless an astute student of history, reading voraciously on a number of historical topics, and more than made up for any limitations through honesty, resilience, firmness of conviction, and the willingness to accept responsibility captured so succinctly by the nameplate on his desk: "The buck stops here!"

Harry S. Truman remains one of the most admired presidents of all time. He was viewed by contemporaries after his presidency as a mediocre leader, but has benefited from the passing of years; scholars now recognize the wisdom of his many tough decisions. He was ranked fifth in a 2000 C-SPAN presidential poll. In the words of Dr. Ken Hechler, former aide to Truman, "He never lost the common touch and was determined to use the awesome power of the presidency to help bring peace and justice to the average people all over the world."[15]

NOTES

[1] Robert H. Ferrell, *Harry S. Truman and the Modern American Presidency* (Boston: Little, Brown, 1983), 6.

[2] See Robert H. Ferrell, ed., *Dear Bess: The Letters from Harry to Bess Truman, 1910–1959* (New York: Harper & Row, 1983).

[3] Richard Lawrence Miller, *Truman: The Rise to Power* (New York: McGraw-Hill, 1986), 260–61; and David McCullough, *Truman* (New York: Simon & Schuster, 1992), 153.

[4] Statement of the President, 6 August 1945. *Public Papers of the Presidents of the United States: Harry S. Truman, 1945* (Washington DC: Government Printing Office, 1961), 199.

[5] George Kennan's infamous telegram outlining the intentions of the Soviets was written on 22 February 1946. See George F. Kennan, *Memoirs* (1967; repr., New York: Pantheon, 1983), 509–11.

[6] Robert J. Donovan, *Conflict and Crisis: The Presidency of Harry S. Truman, 1945–1948* (New York: W. W. Norton, 1977).

[7] Special Message to the Congress, 12 March 1947. *Public Papers of the Presidents of the United States: Harry S. Truman, 1947* (Washington DC: Government Printing Office, 1963), 178–79.

[8] See *The Papers of George C. Marshall* (Baltimore: Johns Hopkins University, 1982).

[9] Special Message to the Congress, 6 September 1945. *Public Papers of the Presidents of the United States: Harry S. Truman, 1945* (Washington DC: Government Printing Office, 1961), 269.

[10] Michael R. Gardner, *Harry Truman and Civil Rights: Moral Courage and Political Risks* (Carbondale, IL: Southern Illinois University Press, 2002); and Miller, *Truman*, 327.

[11] Special Message to the Congress, 2 February 1948. *Public Papers of the Presidents of the United States: Harry S. Truman, 1948* (Washington DC: Government Printing Office, 1964), 121–22.

[12] Margaret Truman, *Harry S. Truman* (New York: William Morrow, 1973), 527.

[13] Harry S. Truman, *Mr. Citizen* (New York: Bernard Geis, 1960).

[14]See Harry S. Truman, *Memoirs,* 2 vols. (Garden City, NY: Double-day, 1955–56).

[15]In 2000, C-SPAN conducted a survey of presidential historians to rank the presidents on ten qualities of presidential leadership. Truman was rated fifth. Ken Hechler, *Working with Truman* (New York: Putnam, 1982), 283.

TRUMAN IN KEY WEST

Robert J. Wolz

On 13 June 2003, a distinguished group of former Truman staff members, presidential and military scholars, a former national security advisor, and throngs of interested well wishers gathered in Key West, Florida, at the Harry S. Truman Little White House. They came for a symposium to honor the fiftieth anniversary of the end of Harry Truman's presidency. But why Key West? The island was the home of the "winter White House" used by President Truman for 175 days during his administration. Why Truman came to Key West is a bit more complex, but the quick answer is because of the tropical climate and secure location.

The U.S. Navy had had a presence in Key West since 1823, when the city sought protection from approximately two thousand Caribbean-based pirates who were attacking the shipping lanes between Cuba and the United States. At the time, Key West was called the "Gibraltar of America,"[1] as the Gulf of Mexico and Atlantic Ocean intersect at Key West and all trade going north, south, or west had to sail past Key West. Commodore David Porter established a base to supply ships and to serve as headquarters for his West Indian Anti-Piracy Squadron. The campaign was successful, and the city of Key West was incorporated in 1828.

The region's military importance was again noted as Florida passed Acts of Secession in 1861. Key West, with a presence of both the U.S. Army and Navy, remained under federal control throughout the Civil War[2] and served as the headquarters of the East Gulf Blockade Squadron. A total of 191 blockade-runners were captured and detained in Key West, an action credited with shortening the Civil War.

After the Civil War, Key West prospered with the salvaging of ships and the introduction of the cigar manufacturing industry

23

from Cuba. In the 1870s, it was one of the wealthiest cities in the United States on a per capita basis and had the highest population of cities in the state of Florida. The city's naval station served as a repair facility during the late nineteenth century. Despite its prosperity, Key West was not always the paradise it has become known as. In 1878, a disgruntled officer wrote, "there are no residences belonging to the Navy, and there are no fit boarding houses in the town, married officers are compelled to rent houses and keep up their own establishments."[3]

HISTORY OF THE FACILITY

In 1889, the Navy finally authorized construction of Quarters A and B, which would one day become the "Little White House." Architect George McKay designed a two-story frame duplex to house the naval station commandant and paymaster. New York contractor Rowland Robbins, who had the low bid of $7,489 for this 8,700-square-foot Victorian home, began construction on 15 January 1890.[4] Lieutenant Commander J. K. Winn, the naval station commander from 1877 to1883 and from 1885 to 1895, wrote on 17 May 1890: "I like the location very much and I believe the houses will be very comfortable, they are certainly very pretty and make an excellent appearance."[5]

In the mid-1890s, the entire Atlantic Fleet was stationed in Key West. On 15 February 1898, the USS *Maine* set sail on her historic voyage from Key West to Havana, Cuba, to protect Americans from growing hostilities between the Spanish government in Cuba and the revolutionaries fighting for independence. The explosion and sinking of the *Maine* brought the United States into the Spanish-American War. Key West served as a major point of demarcation throughout the war.

The year 1906 saw major expansion of the base, with numerous new facilities being constructed. The Key West Naval Station was named the headquarters of the Seventh Naval District, which encompassed all naval activities within the state of Florida. The new commandant, Rear Admiral Lucian Young, arrived in 1911[6] and decided the size of the facility and rooms were not practical. He therefore combined both dwellings into a single house known as Quarters A (the Commandant's House). A submarine base and naval air station were later developed. The building's long history

Little White House, Key West, Florida, 1948. (LWH)

of important guests began when inventor Thomas Edison[7] resided at Quarters A for six months in 1918 as a guest of the Navy.

During World War II, Key West Naval Station became one of the largest experimental bases on the East Coast. The ideal tropical climate allowed for year-round training. The Fleet Sonar School, located in Key West, brought numerous American and Allied sailors to train in submarine detection. An underwater explosives school, underwater divers school, and underwater explosives development schools were all operating on the island. Pilots were training in seaplanes and carrier aircraft. Cruisers, destroyers, submarine tenders, and minesweepers plied the surrounding waters. Thus, training was being conducted underwater, on the surface, and in the air all at the same time at the bustling naval station. In addition, a number of top secret projects were undertaken at the naval station.

With the end of the wartime, the base was downsized, and the commands of the air station and submarine base were combined by Fleet Admiral Chester W. Nimitz. The new commandant considered Quarters A too large, and the building remained unoccupied.

Truman leaving for a walk from the Little White House. From left to right: Truman, Admiral Robert Dennison, General Harry Vaughan, Margaret Truman, John Steelman, David DeLloyd, 29 November 1949. (U.S. Navy/courtesy LWH)

TRUMAN COMES TO KEY WEST

In November 1946, President Harry S. Truman had just completed nineteen demanding months in office. The decision to drop the atomic bomb, the conclusion of World War II, the daunting tasks of rebuilding Japan and Europe, and the conversion of the nation from wartime production to a peacetime economy had taken their toll on the president's health. A few months earlier, he had attempted a vacation on board the USS *Williamsburg* (AGC-369), the presidential yacht, but this had to be cut short. The president wrote to his wife, Bess, on 22 August 1946, "The Maine coast cruise ended in a blow up. Everybody and his brother whom I didn't want to see tried by every hook or crook to rope me into letting him come aboard or having me be seen with him. So I just cancelled the trip."[8]

Dr. Wallace Graham, the president's physician, was alarmed at his patient's health and ordered the president to take a warm vacation with a minimum of distractions. Admiral Chester W. Nimitz immediately suggested the Commandant's Quarters on the Key West Naval Station. The climate was warm and the site offered maximum security and complete privacy for the president. Earle Adams, a local news reporter, speculated that the real reason might be that Nimitz wanted the president to be favorably impressed with the Navy's experimental operations and thereby build support for naval appropriations.[9]

Soon after Truman arrived for his first Key West vacation, he wrote to Bess:

> This place is what I hoped it would be and what I was certain it would not be. I'm in a house built on a Southern plan with galleries all around, upstairs and down. It is the house of the commandant of the submarine base. They have no commandant at present so I'm not ranking anyone out of his house.[10]

Truman described his routine in Key West as follows:

> I have arranged a schedule so that I get up at 7:30 (two hours later than I usually do), go over and have a swim, have breakfast at nine and then go to a nice sand beach a half mile away and get sun and sea water. Come back at noon, have lunch at one and then a nap and sit around and talk until dinner at seven, go to bed when I get ready and then do it over. I've just returned from the beach after trying out the schedule and my cough and cold are nearly gone already.[11]

The president could rest, swim in the warm waters, and walk around the base with complete security and privacy. He inspected the air station and submarine base and enjoyed being a tourist. On 21 November 1946, the president and his party of twenty-two boarded the captured German submarine U 2513 and set sail. According to the trip log, reporters were barred from the trip "because of many secret experimental devices installed on board."[12] While sailing, the submarine commenced a dive to 440 feet.[13] Even though this marked the first submarine dive by any American president, the log stated that, "At no time was the slightest apprehension felt by any member of our party for his safety."[14] Other activities included trips to Fort Jefferson and deep-sea fishing. The president was completely rejuvenated by his visit to Key West and, when ask by the press, he promised to return for additional Key West vacations.

In one sense, President Truman became Key West's biggest promoter of tourism. Harold Laubcher of the local Chamber of

Commerce was quoted in the *Key West Citizen,* "As a result of President Truman's coming here for a week, giving Key West nationwide publicity, additional hundreds of persons from all over the country are likely to be here during the winter season."[15] An economic boom occurred for the entire state.

The *Key West Citizen* quoted the president as he completed his first vacation on 23 November 1946 as saying, "I loved it here." "Will you come back and see us, Mr. President?" asked City Commissioner Louis Carbonell. "You bet I will," Truman replied warmly. "You can't keep me away."[16]

The president had planned a Caribbean vacation to begin on 8 March 1947 that would include a brief stay in Key West and a fifteen-day sail on the *Williamsburg*. An Associated Press release of 7 March stated, "The White House announced that the president's Caribbean vacation had been postponed because of developments." While the White House did not reveal what those developments were, it was generally recognized to mean the growing crisis in Greece. The Associated Press added on 8 March 1947, "Truman sat in the White House, rather than in Key West, weighing the most momentous decision since war's end— whether to reshape historic American foreign policy by calling for the direct intervention in the internal affairs of Greece."[17]

Communist-backed rebels were threatening civil war in both Greece and Turkey. Britain was disengaging its influence from the region by withdrawing 40,000 troops and ending their foreign aid to these nations; as a result, the governments in Greece, Turkey, and Iran were in danger of collapsing. President Truman addressed Congress in early March 1947 asking for $400 million in military and economic aid to the three countries. This major relief effort initiated what became known as the Truman Doctrine, and marked the beginning of a new foreign policy for the United States.

The events leading up to this speech were exhausting. Dr. Graham told United Press International that Truman had "positive instructions for absolute rest."[18] The following day, 13 March 1947, the president left for Key West and wrote to his daughter, Margaret:

> We had a pleasant flight from Washington. Your old Dad slept for 750 or 800 miles—three hours, and we were traveling from 250 to 300 miles an hour. No one, not even me (your mother would say) knew how very tired and worn to a frazzle the

Chief Executive had become. This terrible decision I had to make has been over my head for about six weeks.[19]

Arriving for his second visit to Key West, the president said to Key West mayor William Demerett, "I told you I would be back. This is my favorite vacation spot."[20] Truman wrote to Bess, "I am getting some much needed rest and already feel and look much better."[21]

Special conferences took up much of this second vacation. The president received reports from Secretary of State George Marshall on Russia's reaction to the Truman Doctrine and had meetings with Paul Porter, special envoy to Greece. Truman was in constant contact with Washington in regard to the Truman Doctrine. Congress took a bipartisan stand and supported the president, as did most Americans. This allowed Truman to enjoy some relaxation while on his Key West vacation.

His third visit in December 1947 followed the now-standard routine. Mrs. Truman saw the president and staff off from the Washington airport. The flight lasted about three and a half hours and landed at Boca Chica Naval Air Station, where military and local officials welcomed the president. His motorcade then traveled down the overseas highway to Key West. The December 1947 log described the scene:

> The route was spotted with groups of smiling citizens, including about 3,000 school children who were out to welcome the President back to Key West for another vacation. On entering the city the President took the position atop the back of the rear seat so that he could better acknowledge the greetings of the populace.[22]

Upon the president's arrival at the submarine base, he received full military honors, with 450 enlisted men in dress white uniforms "manning the rails." The party was assigned quarters and the president telephoned his wife to indicate his safe arrival. Usually he and his party would change into lightweight vacation clothes and the vacation would begin. *Miami Herald* columnist Earle Adams put it this way:

> The job of the United States President is an exacting and tiresome one even in tranquil times. The constant strain saps up the energy of the nation's chief executive. Mr. Truman is no exception, but one thing is a certainty, he is determined to get away

President Truman admires a shirt given to him by Seminole Chief William McKinley Osceola at the dedication of the Everglades National Park, 6 December 1947. (U.S. Navy/courtesy TPL, 66-649)

from Washington and back down here whenever he finds himself in need of rest.[23]

The presidential trip log states that "as the trip to Key West had been planned solely for rest and relaxation, the local officials had been asked specifically not to plan any official entertainment or receptions for the President."[24]

On 6 December 1947, the president took a daylong trip to Naples and Everglade City, Florida, where he dedicated the Everglades National Park in a ceremony attended by 5,000 people, including 150 members of the Seminole tribe. The Everglades National Park became the nation's third largest park (only Yellowstone and Mount McKinley were larger). The president was concerned with environmental issues and with the conservation of Florida's "river of grass," as the Everglades is often called. The president himself drove his party back to Naples to board the plane by which they returned to the Little White House.[25] These first visits to Key West were brief periods of relaxation for Truman, but the remarkable effects on the president did not go unnoticed.

A WORKING WHITE HOUSE

The president continued to use Quarters A much as later presidents would use Camp David: as a place to relax and restore body and mind. But unlike Camp David, the Little White House, as Quarters A became known, was the functioning seat of government. The president conducted the affairs of state from his Key West vacation spot. National and international leaders met with the president, correspondence arrived in quantity every few days and was handled, and legislation was enacted. On 28 February 1948, the president, writing to Mrs. Truman, confirmed the use of the Little White House as a functioning White House: "Have been resting well, but the work comes along just the same. I've been reading and signing messages, executive orders, statements, letters etc. at the usual rate."[26]

President Truman used the Little White House for a total of 175 days during his presidency, from 17 November 1946 to 27 March 1952. The relaxed, isolated nature of the Little White House provided opportunities for maximum work with minimum interruptions. The president found this arrangement extremely useful in conducting the affairs of state.

The fourth trip to Key West allowed President Truman to combine his Key West vacation with a goodwill mission to Puerto Rico, the Virgin Islands, and Guantanamo Bay, Cuba. Truman received and carefully reviewed the text of a U.S. policy address on the Palestine refugees while in Key West. The president may have officially been on vacation, but his diplomatic work continued. The trip log noted: "The weather was perfect for a vacation and full opportunity was taken for rest and relaxation."[27]

Press conferences were usually held on the lawn of the Little White House each Thursday, and the president's press secretary held daily news briefings, fending off hot topics with "no comment" or "I don't know."[28] On one such occasion, the public was informed that "the Little White House at Key West confirmed that the President has received a letter direct from Chiang Kai-shek, president of the Chinese government," asking for direct United States military and economic aid against the Chinese Communists.[29] The president's staff confirmed that "Defense Secretary James V. Forrestal will fly here from Washington to talk with President Truman, probably about critical Asiatic and European affairs."[30]

In spite of the official workload he addressed while "on vacation," Truman was not eager to leave Key West. The president wrote to Bess on 4 March 1948, "The weather here is ideal. It is hell to have to go back to slavery [the Washington White House] and the bickerings that I'll have to face from now on, but it must be done."[31] The next day, the president returned to Washington.

Fortunately, Commander William Rigdon, President Truman's assistant naval aide, kept careful logs of each of the president's trips, detailing all the daily activities. A careful reading of his logs reveals the transition of the Little White House from a brief vacation spot to the functioning White House, and provides historians with rich insights into the Little White House and Truman's presidency. Commander Rigdon noted:

> On our first visit, in 1946, the President's needs were provided by sixteen persons, including cooks, stewards, clerical and communications personnel, but not including the ever-present force of Secret Service agents. On the eleventh and final outing there, in 1952, a second house in addition to the Little White House and the Presidential yacht was needed to accommodate the fifty-seven staffers and service assistants.[32]

But there was always time for rest and relaxation, and a little time for fun. The president wrote to Bess on 29 November 1949, "The sun shines with terrific force down here. My face and head are as red as a beet, but the rest of me is brown except for a strip around the middle which is white."[33] Truman's time in Key West was described as follows:

> The President liked to wear colorful caps and sports shirts at Key West. Both came as gifts in such numbers that they spilled over into the supplies of staffers and reporters. Incoming shirts, caps, fishing gear or whatnot would be opened on a large table, where everyone was free to take his choice.[34]

On several occasions, the president's staff at the Little White House joined in the fun with a "loud shirt" contest. President Truman's secretary notes in December 1949:

> The two great social events of the vacation at Key West were a loud shirt contest and the impersonation of the President. The Presidential assistants outdid each other in the lurid shirt deal. Bill Hassett, the kindly White House veteran, wore a pink and white check. But Matt Connolly, the President's No. 1 assistant,

won hands down. A special shirt was flown in from Mexico. It was a flaming red silk with an Aztec calendar done in black and yellow.[35]

What had begun as a publicity stunt by Royal Palm Sportswear of Miami became the Key West uniform of the president, his staffers, and even the newspaper reporters. Truman looked like he was on vacation. Upon arriving in Key West, the president would change from the more formal business suit of Washington DC to a tropical shirt with khaki slacks and a golf cap or pith helmet. Some other hats even came complete with attached sunglasses. Truman always carried a cane, but it was not used for stability; it was an accessory, as Truman loved to walk ten blocks at a brisk 120 paces a minute each morning. One might conclude that he had invented "power walking."

Walking and swimming were his two favorite forms of exercise. The Key West Naval Station provided the security and privacy

President Truman and General Harry Vaughan in Key West, ca. November 1951. (U.S. Navy/ courtesy TPL, 58-785)

for his walks. Once, while walking around the base, the president stopped at the enlisted men's mess and hopped into line. Imagine the looks on his fellow diners' faces! Occasionally, the president would venture into town, usually accompanied by a small handful of Secret Service agents. On one such excursion, local restaurateur Sebastian Cabrera offered the president and his staff a cup of coffee at his Caribe Restaurant on Front Street. When the president said he would take a rain check, the Secret Service checked out the facility. It passed inspection: "The door opened and in walked a grinning customer in a green billed fishing cap and colorful sport shirt." "I'm here," said the president as he climbed up on a counter stool, "to get that cup of coffee you promised me." The president paid Cabrera with an autographed one-dollar bill. "This ought to be a profitable cup of coffee," the president told Cabrera, "because a lot of people think this signature is valuable."[36] The framed dollar was displayed in the restaurant for years until a late-night robbery claimed it. The coffee cup was donated to the local historical society.

November 1948 saw the president and his family come to the Little White House to recover from the hard-fought political campaign in which Truman had a surprise upset against Republican Tom Dewey. The president had traveled over 31,000 miles that summer campaigning on his whistle-stop train tour. President Truman wrote to his sister, Mary, on 11 November 1948, "I didn't know I was so tired until I sat down."[37] This was a victory celebration and numerous well-wishers joined the president in Key West. Margaret Truman wrote in her biography of her father, "Mother and I joined Dad in Key West for his vacation. We needed a rest almost as much as he did."[38] The entourage included Truman's staff and advisors to work on the administration's program and on the inaugural address. Vice President-elect Alben Barkley and Speaker of the House Sam Rayburn also joined the president. The previous three weeks had been extremely busy for all of the presidential party.

THE LITTLE WHITE HOUSE

The November 1948 trip also marked Mrs. Truman's first visit to the Little White House. In the past, the presidential visits had been men-only affairs. Margaret Truman wrote, "Mother saw it as an all-male setup and thought Dad would have a better time horsing around with Charlie Ross (his press secretary) and Admiral Leahy (his naval aide), playing poker, and drinking a little bourbon beyond the range of her critical eye."[39]

Captain Cecil Adell, commanding Key West Station, and Rear Admiral J. J. Manning, USN Chief of the Bureau of Yards and Docks, realized that Mrs. Truman would be coming more often since Truman had just been reelected to a full four-year term, so they decided the Little White House should be redecorated in a style more suitable for the First Family. They hired Miami-based interior decorator Haygood Lassiter to completely redecorate the house and to make some structural improvements. Some floors were leveled or ramped to eliminate deep steps, and several upstairs bedrooms were enlarged by absorbing the porches on the east side of the house into the floor plan. The south porch—which the president used as a recreation room—was enlarged to accommodate the increasing number of staffers coming to Key West. Its furnishings included a prized solid mahogany poker table presented to the president by the naval base's cabinet shop.

The contract awarded $35,000 to the interior designer for the renovation, and all the rooms received a fresh new look described by Lassiter as "Georgetownish." Comfortable reading chairs with good lighting filled the spaces in this pre-television home. The radio-phonograph in the living room was a popular diversion for the president and his staff, who enjoyed prizefights, sporting events, and music. The president often worked while listening to Chopin recordings. It was here in March 1947 that President Truman heard his daughter's first broadcast performance, singing with the Detroit Symphony.

Leather-inlaid mahogany tables and Hepplewhite-style furnishings brought a new elegance. The colors were those popular in the 1940s: avocado green, grays, lime green, deep blues, gray greens, tomato red, and bright yellow. The designs reflected a tropical atmosphere, especially the floral and banana leaf prints and natural jute fibers.

In less than four months the remodeling was completed. When the presidential party returned on 16 March 1949, the president was delighted. He wrote to Bess,

> They have fixed you up a palatial bedroom next to mine. You've never seen a nicer one. The place is all redecorated. The porches have been leveled up so there are no steps from the

*The First Family enjoying the warm Key West weather on the Little White House
lawn, November 1948. (U.S. Navy/courtesy TPL, 74-345)*

dining room—new furniture and everything. I've a notion to
move the Capitol to Key West and just stay.[40]

The remodeling made the Little White House much more pleas-
ant, but the president's workload did not decrease. On 15 March
1949, "Lieutenant Levy delivered three sacks of official mail at the
Little White House." Two days later, the trip log records "Chief
Ship's Clerk Prophet arrived at the Little White House at 2:30
p.m., with four sacks of official mail."[41]

Among the many distinguished guests the Little White House
hosted were Chief Justice Fred Vinson and General George Marshall, who vacationed with the president. Secretary of the Treasury John Snyder and Budget Director Frank Pace Jr. also flew
into Key West for meetings with the president. Distance was no
obstacle to the functioning of the presidency. These informal
meetings gave the president a chance to discuss pressing issues
with high-ranking officials in a relaxed atmosphere, as when
President Truman asked Judge Vinson to consider running for
president for the 1952 election.[42] At the end of November and for
a large part of December 1949, the First Family and a sizeable
entourage of staffers vacationed at the Little White House. The
routine was described thus:

About 10 a.m. each morning all hands assembled at the Little White House and left from there in a group for the beach, where they spent the forenoon. The afternoons, generally, were free for rest. However, considerable staff work was accomplished on the messages delivered to Congress the first week of January 1950. The President also worked for an hour or longer most evenings after he retired to his quarters, and cleared up a backlog of official papers which he took south with him.[42]

Under the shade of coconut and cork trees on the lawn of the winter White House on Wednesday, December 7th [1949], the President and 16 aides held their first staff meeting on the forthcoming State of the Union message. The conference lasted one hour and forty five minutes. It was a round table discussion devoted almost wholly to Mr. Truman's domestic program.[44]

Picnics were held on the Little White House lawn. The fare was an all-American menu of hot dogs, hamburgers, and corn on the cob all served with formal china and silver. Even in Key West, the president could not escape the formality of the White House. To this point, the president had always flown to Key West for vacations either on the *Sacred Cow* (C-54) or the *Independence* (DC-6), the forerunners to Air Force One. In March 1950, the president decided to sail to Key West on the *Williamsburg*. A course was laid contouring the coastline to offer smoother sailing. However, on 13 March near Cape Hatteras, "rough seas were encountered all day. From 3:25 p.m. on, conditions were such that it was desirable for the *Williamsburg* to proceed at two-thirds speed.... The president and most members of the party stuck to their quarters all day. Attendance at meals was light."[45] Once past Cape Hatteras, the seas became calm for an enjoyable sail, but this was the only time the president sailed to Key West. After this voyage,

> the President's first act on reaching the Little White House was to telephone Mrs. Truman (in Washington) to report his safe arrival. He then went to his desk in the living room where he worked on a batch of mail that had been flown down from Washington the day before. Included in the papers signed at this time were S.471, S.576, S.1310, S.1552, S.1737, S.1764, S.2125, S.2429, S.2441, HR 2023 and HR 6670.[46]

The log from this trip reflects the official nature of the Little White House. The naval station newspaper, *The Key Outpost,* observed,

"All during the presidential visit much time was spent signing bills, appointments, and making nominations to fill government posts."[47] Indeed, the routine remained the same as in previous visits. Commander Rigdon, in the official log, writes:

> Those members of the party who did not care to attend the movies gathered on the south porch after dinner for informal discussions or a game of cards. All was not play, however, for in between periods of relaxation the President and members of his staff transacted a considerable amount of official business.[48]

There were numerous critics charging that the president spent too much time away from Washington, but a few like David Lawrence of the *New York Herald Tribune* defended Truman, writing in his 20 March 1950 column:

> President Truman has found here rest and seclusion—a chance to think through some of the major problems that bother him. He gets a vacation, of course, from the pressures of a daily calling list and from the hour-by-hour demands on his time from heads of departments and government agencies. But the task of being President never ceases for a moment.
>
> Life goes on almost exactly as it does in Washington. The press corps is here…just as curious and persevering in representing the people's interest.
>
> In back of the President is an efficient staff in Washington, which sifts the important from the unimportant before sending down a pouch of mail. Anything that comes here for action is of topmost significance—and much of what is done here isn't publicized at all.
>
> The President can send for anyone and bring him here by air in a few hours for a conference. He can do business by telephone if he wishes to work faster than the airplane can carry his letters and orders.
>
> Even the idea of a three way hook-up with two or three other persons participating in a telephone conference has been developed for the President's benefit—and he has frequently taken advantage of this mechanical set-up.[49]

Some of President Truman's staff confided that they worked harder in Key West than they did in Washington. Captain (later Admiral) Robert L. Dennison said, "We had to work like hell and still not give the appearance of working, so it was really hell for

President Truman working in the Little White House living room, 8 March 1951. (U.S. Navy/courtesy TPL, 66-1124)

all of us, but we had our regard in knowing that (Truman) was really having a great time."[50] Ample time in Key West was devoted to work, but the president also took time to reflect on his future plans:

> In mid-November 1951, during a brief vacation in Key West, Truman gathered [his senior staff members] about the poker table on the porch at the Little White House to read aloud the statement he had written on April 12, 1950, and that he was planning to release in the coming spring, in April 1952, well in advance of the Democratic National Convention. He was not running again; but for the next five months, he cautioned them, there must be utmost secrecy. He was only telling them now, he explained, so they could start making their own plans.[51]

No staff member ever leaked this information. The press continued to speculate if President Truman sat on the beach pondering whether he should run or not.

The last visits in 1951 and 1952 were during the Korean War. As might be expected, the Little White House was even more involved as the site of government activity, and was described as follows:

> Strict security was observed throughout the period of the visit. In addition to an increased Secret Service detail about the Little White House, an armed guard was maintained around the house by the Marine Corps personnel, and a continuous watch was kept at the beach used by the President and also at adjacent Fort Taylor.... A special pass, signed by the Naval Base security officer and countersigned by a representative of the Secret Service, was required for one to be permitted to enter or leave the grounds of the Little White House.[52]

The Little White House clerical staff was increased by three stenographers. On 5 March 1951 while at the beach, the president had a conference call with Vice President Barkley, Speaker of the House Sam Rayburn, Senate Majority Leader E. W. McFarland, and House Majority Leader John W. McCormack. This is but one of several conference calls that the president held while in Key West. In addition, paperwork continued to occupy a significant amount of his time.

> Wednesday night (March 12, 1952), Mr. Truman had to sign his name over 200 times to public documents, a pouch having arrived from Washington with the usual flow of public papers with which he had to deal. He worked on the new papers before and after breakfast, took a swim and a walk Thursday morning, then got back to work in the afternoon.[53]

The conduct of the Korean War continued to demand Truman's attention. The losses in Korea were staggering. President Truman, the Joint Chiefs of Staff, and many in the Congress feared a third world war would result, with the Soviet Union joining the Chinese and North Koreans. The headstrong General Douglas MacArthur, a World War II hero and the Allied Commander in Korea, added to Truman's troubles by issuing inflammatory declarations from the front lines. In October 1950, President Truman had met with the general on Wake Island where an understanding was reached that Washington would issue any policy statements.

The March 1951 trip to Key West was no vacation at all. Truman staffers, the Pentagon, and the State Department felt the time was right to prepare a ceasefire proposal. On 20 March 1951, the president submitted a draft proposal to the other seventeen nations with troops in Korea. The president returned to Washington on the night of 22 March; however, General MacArthur, on 23 March (Washington DC time) tried to seize the initiative with his own statement threatening to expand the war, in effect saying that the United States was going to attack China.[54] President Truman wrote in his memoirs:

> It was an act totally disregarding all directives to abstain from any declarations on foreign policy. It was an open defiance of my orders as President and as Commander in Chief. This was a challenge to the President under the Constitution. It also flouted the policy of the United Nations.[55]

The president relieved General MacArthur of command in Korea and replaced him with General Matthew Ridgway. Thousands of Americans could not believe the president would do such a thing to a beloved war hero like MacArthur. Most historians today agree that replacing MacArthur was one of President Truman's greatest opportunities to demonstrate the American principal that the civilian government has supremacy over the military.

With increased tension due to the Korean War, classified communication to Key West was handled by duplex radio tele-type via the USS *Williamsburg* and the U.S. Navy. This system allowed messages to be simultaneously sent and received. A backup security system was established between the Key West Naval Station, the Navy, and the White House. Regular telephone traffic totaled 10,366 minutes during the 8 November–9 December 1951 visit. Ticker tape news service was also added to keep the president informed of late-breaking news.

THE LITTLE WHITE HOUSE'S LEGACY

Truman's eleventh and final presidential visit to Key West was from 7 March to 27 March 1952. During this visit, President Truman held a press conference on the north lawn.

> Newsreel, television and press photographers crowded up as he sat down in a white wicker lawn chair. …He read two prepared statements and the questions started. …His retrospection came near the end of the session. "The best any president can do is endeavor to make the executive branch of government run in an efficient manner," the president said in response to a question. "No president can be evaluated," he added, "during his term in office or during the 25 years after it. That takes a projected survey." When asked what he believed his administration

The Little White House has been the site of many diplomatic meetings. Here, U.S. Secretary of State Colin Powell meets with President Heydar Aliyev of Azerbaijan, President Robert Kocharian of Armenia, and others, 4 April 2001. (Andy Newman/ courtesy LWH)

would be remembered for he said, "I hope that it will be remembered for its sincere effort for world peace. If we accomplish that and get through this era without a third world war, that will be what it will be remembered for."[56]

This visit was the last vacation when President Truman used the Little White House as his presidential retreat. The following month, he announced his intention not to seek reelection. But, because of his presence, Key West had become "Trumanized." By action of the City Commission, Division Street was renamed Truman Avenue; the County School Board followed by changing the name of the Division Street School to Truman Elementary School.

Later, Presidents Dwight Eisenhower and John F. Kennedy would use the Little White House for limited official functions. Jimmy Carter visited the facility after his presidency and Secretary of State Colin Powell selected the Little White House as the site for a diplomatic summit in 2001. The U.S. Navy resumed use of the building as the command headquarters for the Key West Naval Station until 1974, when the base was decommissioned. The building and grounds opened as a state historic site in April 1991 and now welcome 60,000 visitors each year. The Little White House continues to be a site used for diplomatic functions, a tribute to the man who longed for lasting peace in the world.

NOTES

[1] Jefferson Browne, *Key West, The Old and the New* (1912; repr., Gainesville, FL: Bicentennial Floridiana Facsimile Series, 1973), 213.

[2] Browne, *Key West,* 214.

[3] Lt. Cmdr. J. K. Winn to Capt. A. W. Johnson, May 1883. Reprinted in "Naval Station Key West 1883." *Florida Keys Sea Heritage Journal* (Winter 1999/2000): 12–13.

[4] U.S. Navy, Bureau of Yards and Docks, *US Navy Acceptance of Bid for Officers Quarters at Key West, Fla.,* 15 January 1890.

[5] J. K. Winn to U.S. Navy, Bureau of Yards and Docks, 17 May 1890. Little White House.

[6] Browne, *Key West,* 75.

[7] Robert Holgrim (scientist who worked with Thomas Edison in Key West). Interview by Robert J. Wolz, 5 December 1999.

[8] Margaret Truman, *Harry S. Truman* (New York: William Morrow, 1973), 334.

[9] Earle Adams, "Truman Discovered Key West By Purpose," *Miami Herald,* 7 December 1947.

[10] Harry S. Truman to Bess Truman, 18 November 1946, in *Dear Bess: The Letters From Harry to Bess Truman 1910–1959,* ed. Robert H. Ferrell (New York: W. W. Norton, 1983), 540.

[11] M. Truman, *Harry S. Truman,* 324.

[12] William M. Rigdon, *Log of President Truman's [First] Vacation Trip to Key West, Florida, November 17–23, 1946,* 11. Truman Presidential Library.

[13] John Vosburgh, "President Submerges 440 Feet," *Key West Citizen,* 21 November 1946.

[14] Rigdon, *Log of the President's [First] Trip to Key West,* 11.

[15] "Many Tourists Arriving in Key West, Chamber of Commerce Register Shows," *Key West Citizen,* 18 November 1946.

[16] John Vosburgh, "I Loved It Here," *Key West Citizen,* 23 November 1946.

[17] Associated Press release, 8 March 1947.

[18] United Press International release, 12 March 1947.

[19] Roy Jenkins, *Truman* (New York: Harper & Row,1986), 102.

[20] Earle Adams, "Truman Lands in Key West," *Miami Herald,* 13 March 1947.

[21] Harry S. Truman to Bess Truman, 15 March 1947, in *Dear Bess,* ed. Ferrell, 544.

[22] William M. Rigdon, *Log of the President's Third Visit to Key West, Florida, December 3–8, 1947,* 4. Truman Presidential Library.

[23] Earle Adams, "Key West Truman's Ideal Spot," *Miami Herald,* 23 March 1947.

[24] Rigdon, *Log of the President's Third Visit to Key West,* 5.

[25] William M. Rigdon, *Log of the President's Second Visit to Key West, March 12–19, 1947*, 15–17. Truman Presidential Library.

[26] Harry S. Truman to Bess Truman, 28 February 1948, in *Dear Bess*, ed. Ferrell, 553.

[27] William M. Rigdon, *Log of the President's Trip to Puerto Rico, the Virgin Islands, Guantanamo Bay, Cuba, and [Fourth] Key West, Florida, 20 February–5 March 1948*, 42. Truman Presidential Library.

[28] Paul White, "Little White House on Florida Island," *Tampa Sunday Tribune*, 2 December 1951.

[29] Paul R. Leach, "New Force to Cover Evacuation," *Miami Herald*, 18 November 1948.

[30] Earle Adams, "Cabinet Job May Be Decided," *Miami Herald*, 18 November 1948.

[31] Harry S. Truman to Bess Truman, 4 March 1948, in *Letters Home*, ed. Monte M. Poen (Columbia: University of Missouri Press, ca. 1984), 233.

[32] William Rigdon, *The White House Sailor* (Garden City, NY: Doubleday, 1962), 256.

[33] Harry S. Truman to Bess Truman, 29 November 1946, in *Letters Home*, ed. Poen, 230.

[34] Rigdon, *White House Sailor*, 262.

[35] Secretary's Notes, 20 December 1949. *The President's Trip to Key West, Florida, November 28–December 20, 1949*, 14. President's Secretary's Files, Truman Presidential Library.

[36] United Press International, "Key Wester's Unwashed Cup Will Attest: Truman Drank Coffee Here," *Miami Herald*, 28 November 1951.

[37] M. Truman, *Harry S. Truman*, 394.

[38] Ibid., 395.

[39] Margaret Truman, *Bess W. Truman* (New York: Macmillan, 1986), 304.

[40] Harry S. Truman to Bess Truman, 13 March 1949, Files Pertaining to Family Business and Personal Affairs, Truman Presidential Library.

[41] William M. Rigdon, *Log of President Truman's [Sixth] Trip to Key West and Orlando, Florida, 6–19 March 1949*, 52, 57. Truman Presidential Library.

[42] Harry S. Truman to Bess Truman, 6 March 1949. Files Pertaining to Family Business and Personal Affairs, Truman Presidential Library.

[43] William M. Rigdon, *Log of President Truman's [Seventh] Trip to Key West, Florida, 28 November–20 December 1949*, 21. Truman Presidential Library.

[44] Secretary's Notes, 7 December 1949. *The President's Trip to Key West, Florida, November 28–December 20, 1949*, 7. President's Secretary's Files, Truman Presidential Library.

[45] William M. Rigdon, *Log of President Truman's Eighth Visit to Key West, Florida, 12 March–10 April 1950*, 5. Truman Presidential Library.

[46] Rigdon, *Log of President's Eighth Visit to Key West*, 11.

[47] *Key Outpost* (US Naval Station, Key West, Florida), 14 April 1950.

[48] Rigdon, *Log of President's Eighth Visit to Key West,* 23.

[49] David Lawrence, "Today in Key West," *New York Herald Tribune,* 21 March 1950.

[50] Robert L. Dennison, Interview by Jerry N. Hess, 10 September 1971. Truman Presidential Library.

[51] David McCullough, *Truman* (New York: Simon & Schuster, 1992), 873–74.

[52] William M. Rigdon, *Log of President Truman's Ninth Visit to Key West, Florida, and Ft. Jefferson National Monument, 2–22 March 1951,* 11, 13. Truman Presidential Library.

[53] Secretary's File, 14 March 1952. *The President's Trip to Key West, Florida, March 7–March 29, 1952,* 7. President's Secretary's Files, Truman Presidential Library.

[54] Douglas MacArthur, *Reminiscences* (New York: McGraw-Hill, 1964), 388.

[55] Harry S. Truman. Memoirs. Vol. 2, *Years of Trial & Hope* (New York: Doubleday, 1956), 441–42.

[56] "President Truman Meets the Press," *Key Outpost* (U.S. Naval Station, Key West, Florida), 16 March 1951.

WORKING
FOR
TRUMAN

TRUMAN'S SIX IMMATERIAL LEGACIES

George M. Elsey

The purpose of gathering Truman scholars and former Truman aides at the Truman Legacy Symposium in 2003—and in this book—is to consider our thirty-third president's legacies as they relate to national security. A legacy, according to the *Oxford English Dictionary,* is a "material or immaterial thing handed down by a predecessor."

Government bureaucracies are about the most material things imaginable. Some bureaucracies relating to national security created in the Truman administration are the Department of Defense, the Department of the Air Force, the Central Intelligence Agency, and the National Security Council. Others, not as well known but equally significant, include the National Security Agency and the

Lieutenant George M. Elsey, Captain James K. Vardaman, naval aide to the president, and Ship's Clerk Edwin L. Hoying on the deck of the USS Augusta, *7 August 1945. Elsey and Hoying were the Map Room staffers who accompanied President Truman on his Potsdam trip to maintain the maps and code and decode secret messages. (U.S. Army/courtesy TPL, 63-1453)*

National Science Foundation. Some of these material things—to use that bland dictionary definition of legacy—receive attention from the other contributors to this book, and are quite well known among those chronicling Truman's legacy. By contrast, I shall focus on six immaterial things bequeathed by Harry S. Truman that I regard as meaningful legacies affecting our national security in the past half century.

THE ROLE OF THE VICE PRESIDENT

First, Truman changed forever the role of the vice president. When Harry Truman became president in April 1945 on Franklin Roosevelt's sudden death, he was unprepared for his responsibilities insofar as foreign and military affairs were concerned. FDR had cavalierly ignored all his vice presidents on such matters, as had earlier presidents. Roosevelt's first vice president, John Garner, is quoted as saying of his eight years in the job that it "wasn't worth a bucket of warm spit."[1] (I have heard that Garner actually used a different four-letter word.)

In his first weeks as president, Truman struggled to grasp the world military situation. He worked hard to master the arcane files of Roosevelt's cabled exchanges with Winston Churchill, Joseph Stalin, and Chiang Kai-shek. He was a frequent visitor to the Map Room—the White House intelligence and communication center—where I, a young Naval Reserve officer, was stationed. Because I was intimately familiar with the Churchill-Stalin-Chiang files as well as the records of summit conferences at Casablanca, Quebec, Cairo, Teheran, and Yalta, I was charged with preparing memoranda for the new president summarizing issues that demanded his early attention and about which he had been told nothing—nothing at all—by Roosevelt. Truman admired his predecessor, but he never forgave FDR for failing to entrust his vice president with national security matters that he truly had a "need to know."

There was no constitutional provision in those days for filling a vice presidential vacancy. Truman had to wait until January 1949 before he had a vice president. He then saw to it that Alben Barkley was taken into full confidence on national security matters. Harry Truman deliberately and carefully began the enhancement of the vice presidency from a "bucket of warm...whatever" to the lofty stature in national security matters enjoyed today by Vice President Richard Cheney. A significant legacy indeed!

RESPONDING TO WORLD EVENTS

A second legacy is the pattern Truman set for his successors on how to act when world events require a major change in policy. His approach: do not rush, do not be pushed, consult a wide spectrum of advisors, and take the time to get it right.

Truman sailed in early July 1945 for a conference in Potsdam, Germany, with Churchill and Stalin. I was in his party. I know that he regarded the Soviet Union as a valiant ally and was eager for the Soviets to join with us in the final stages of the war with Japan. (The USSR was still at peace with Japan.) But Soviet aid was not needed; within days of our return home, two atomic bombs brought Japanese surrender.

The president was soon bombarded with conflicting advice. Such influential figures as Eleanor Roosevelt and Henry Wallace (his predecessor as vice president) assured him that he must maintain good relations with the Soviet Union—at all cost. Equally influential advisors warned that the Soviets were danger-ous enemies bent on world domination and must be blocked—at all cost.

Truman refused to make a quick decision. He was cautious and thoughtful. He listened to all whose opinions he valued. In the late summer of 1946, a top-secret study (known later as the Clifford-Elsey Report) summarized multiple examples of Soviet violations of agreements and alarming behavior in sensitive geo-graphic areas. Truman pondered the study but still felt disagree-ments between our two countries could be settled amicably. He did, however, drop consideration of a substantial loan to the Soviet Union comparable to one made earlier to the British. Not until March 1947, when Soviet threats to Greece and Turkey were truly alarming, did Truman announce a new national policy to the Congress— and to the world. "I believe," he said,

> that it must be the policy of the United States to support free peoples who are resisting attempted subjugation by armed minorities or by outside pressures. I believe that we must assist free peoples to work out their own destinies in their own way.

The "Big Three"—Truman, Attlee, and Stalin—with staffs around the conference table, 1 August 1945. Also pictured are Ernest Bevin, James F. Byrnes, Andrei Gromyko, William D. Leahy, and Vyacheslav Molotov. (TPL, 63-1457-21)

I believe that our help should be primarily through economic and financial aid.[2]

It was Truman's long-awaited decision on U.S.–Soviet relations. Although couched in polite language, the President had drawn a firm line that was not to be crossed. Members of the White House staff claimed no credit for the decision—it was Truman's alone—but I was one of the scribblers who shaped the phrases of this statement that guided our country's actions for the next several decades.

What was Truman's lesson for his successors? Just this: When a new direction in national security policy becomes necessary, do not be rushed. Take the time to get it right. Then stick with it!

EQUALITY OF TREATMENT AND OPPORTUNITY

The importance of the third legacy cannot be overstated. On 26 July 1948, Truman issued Executive Order 9981, which declared, "It is...the policy of the President that there shall be equality of treatment and opportunity for all persons in the armed services without regard to race, color, religion, or national origin."[3]

Truman issued the executive order to the open-mouthed astonishment of the military's top brass, to the dismay of political friends who worried about its impact on the upcoming presidential election, to the outrage of citizens in some states and the joy of citizens in others, and to the special gratification of those of us on the White House staff who had been impatient for such action. When it had become obvious that Congress would not act on the president's recommendations as outlined in Truman's bold civil rights message of the preceding February, we had been urging that he use his authority as commander in chief to address the matter. And so he did.

Truman knew the executive order would bring howls of wrath from many quarters and raise hurdles in his bid for reelection in November, but he did what he knew was right. The transition from segregation to integration in the services did not come overnight, nor was it without pain, but this legacy of Truman to his successors has given us a stronger, more just, and more secure United States. We are all indebted to him.

PRIORITY ONE—NATIONAL SECURITY

A fourth legacy Truman learned the hard way is that a president must never be penny-wise and pound-foolish when it comes to national security. Concerned at the size of the national debt, anxious to have a balanced budget, worried about the high level of taxes, and eager to have money for his Fair Deal domestic programs, Truman imposed a dangerously low ceiling on Army, Navy, and Air Force budgets in 1949. His bull-in-a-china-shop secretary of defense, Louis Johnson, went further and slashed items the Joint Chiefs of Staff believed were essential to counter the growing military capabilities of the Soviet Union.

I was back in uniform on temporary duty in the Department of the Navy when Johnson axed the Navy's dream—a new aircraft supercarrier. I experienced firsthand the navy's anger at Johnson's cut and dismay at Truman's seeming indifference to their needs. While at the Department of the Navy, I kept in close touch with my former White House colleagues with whom I knew I would be working again very soon. Through them I learned that the highest levels at the Department of State shared the concerns of the military leadership that our defenses were inadequate for the dangerous world situation. Secretary of State Dean Acheson favored a military buildup. Secretary of Defense Johnson favored more cuts. The two were locked in fierce battle.

Before Truman could resolve the conflict over the proper level of military spending, North Korea invaded South Korea on 25 June 1950. The Truman-Johnson military budgets were scrapped. Johnson was fired in a painful Oval Office confrontation that the badly shaken president described to his press secretary and to me just moments after Johnson stumbled out of the White House.

Before the Korean conflict ended, all the funding that the uniformed military had urged and the Department of State had recommended—and much, much more—was poured into Army, Navy, and Air Force budgets. This legacy, painfully learned by Truman—that domestic considerations must never stand in the way of essential funds for national security—has been taken to heart by most, if not all, presidents since.

THE AUTHORITY OF THE COMMANDER IN CHIEF

A fifth immaterial thing has also proven to be a lasting legacy: Truman demonstrated so forcefully the constitutional authority of the president as commander in chief that there has been no subsequent challenge to it. In 1949, he relieved the chief of naval preparations, Admiral Louis Denfeld, saying: "There is only one way to handle insubordination and that is to put a stop to it." Two years later, Truman fired General of the Army Douglas MacArthur, at the time commanding the army in Korea as well as other forces in the Far East, for flagrantly ignoring a written presidential order. MacArthur had gotten away with insubordination when he was Army Chief of Staff and had ignored an order of President Herbert Hoover. But Truman was not Hoover.

I have an especially sharp memory of the MacArthur dismissal. The specific presidential order MacArthur violated, cited in the congressional hearings that followed his firing, was one sent to military commanders worldwide requiring them to clear with Washington any statement they proposed to make to the press or public relating to foreign policy. The order had been drafted on Sunday afternoon by me (then administrative assistant to the president) and Assistant Secretary of State for Public Affairs Edward Barrett. We were agonizing over MacArthur's latest denunciation of the administration's policy from his headquarters in Tokyo. Ed and I knew that an order sent only to MacArthur to clear his pronouncements with Washington would bring torrents of criticism, especially from his Republican supporters in Congress. An order directed broadly to all overseas commanders would be easier to defend. After Barrett called me Monday morning to report Acheson's hearty approval of the proposed order, I took it into the Oval Office. "Get it out!" was Truman's immediate response.

MacArthur paid the order no heed, keeping up his bitter criticisms without clearing anything with Washington. This insubordination, combined with alarm at his tactics in Korea, was the last

President Truman with General MacArthur on Wake Island, 15 October 1950. (TPL, 67-434)

straw. Truman knew all hell would break loose if he fired the politically ambitious and enormously popular general, but that did not deter him at all. No matter how high the rank or how popular the admiral or general, Truman made it clear that an order from the civilian commander in chief was to be obeyed. No senior military officer since has flouted civilian authority. Truman's legacy goes unchallenged.

PRESIDENTIAL CONTROL OF ATOMIC/NUCLEAR WEAPONS

Perhaps no single decision of Truman's has aroused more controversy through the years, and continues to do so to this day, than his alleged decision while at the Potsdam conference with the British and Soviets to "drop the bomb." The fact is that the final decision resulting in dropping atomic bombs on Hiroshima and Nagasaki was not made in Potsdam, nor was it made by Truman. A joint statement by the American, British, and Chinese governments was issued simultaneously in Washington, London, and Chungking on 26 July 1945 (ten days after a test at Alamogordo, New Mexico, proved that the atomic bomb project was a success). The statement, known as the Potsdam Declaration, called on Japan to surrender its armed forces unconditionally or face utter and prompt destruction. Two days later, Japan responded to the declaration. Prime Minister Kantaro Suzuki said he would treat the declaration with *mokusatsu,* an uncommon word translated as "silent contempt." When Truman was later asked about the Japanese response, he tersely said: "They told me to go to hell!"

Had the Japanese government given any indication it was willing to begin peace talks based on the unconditional surrender of its military, no atomic bombs would have been dropped on a Japanese city. Thus, the final decision that resulted in the tragedies of Hiroshima and Nagasaki was made in Tokyo by the militarists who controlled the Japanese government, not in Potsdam, and not by Truman.

The magnitude of the radiological effects of the bombs was not clearly understood until American scientists and medical personnel were able to visit the sites and until further nuclear tests were carried out on Pacific atolls. That information confirmed Truman's decision that all aspects of atomic energy must remain

Winston Churchill, Harry S. Truman, and Joseph Stalin at Potsdam, 25 July 1945.
(U.S. Army/courtesy TPL, 63-1457-28)

under civilian control and that no atomic weapon could be used without the personal and specific authorization of the president of the United States—a decision that remains in effect today.

In December 1950, when the situation in Korea was at its worst, Truman made a careless remark at a press conference that implied atomic weapons might be used in Korea. In fact, he rejected any such thought. When Air Force Chief of Staff General Hoyt Vandenberg remarked, "If China comes in, that will mean atomic weapons," Truman asked sharply: "Who told you that?" Vandenberg replied, "That's part of our strategic doctrine, sir." Truman responded, "No! Go get a new strategic doctrine!"

When the Chinese did indeed enter Korea in force and General MacArthur cabled Washington suggesting that the U.S. recognize a state of war with China and drop thirty to fifty atomic bombs on Manchurian and Chinese cities, the White House gave his melodramatic cable no consideration at all. The Joint Chiefs of Staff knew Truman's mind.

Truman's ideas—that atomic and nuclear research and development must be controlled by civilian and not military authorities, and that such weapons can be employed only by specific and personal authority of the president—are legacies of profound significance for us and for the world.

These six immaterial things, if we choose to so describe them, deserve to be remembered along with the many other national security legacies of Harry S. Truman. Six memories for me. Six legacies for the country.

NOTES

[1]Otis L. Graham Jr. and Meghan Robinson Wander, eds., *Franklin D. Roosevelt: His Life and Times* (Boston: G.K. Hall, 1985), 154.

[2]Special Message to the Congress, 12 March 1947. *Public Papers of the Pressidents of the United States: Harry S. Truman, 1947* (Washington DC: Government Printing Office, 1963), 178–79.

[3]Executive Order 9981, 26 July 1948. *Code of Federal Regulations: Title 3—The President: 1943–1948 Compilation* (Washington DC: Government Printing Office, 1957), 722.

Remembering Truman

Ken Hechler

My chief claim to fame is that Margaret Truman used to ask her father, "Dad, do you know that the Truman train is the only campaign train that carries its own 'heckler' right on board?" I owe so much to George Elsey and Milton Kayle. Milt was my roommate when we were in Key West over Thanksgiving of 1951, and George was my boss in the White House and gave me all the good ideas that I had—I used to claim them even though George originated them. George also had the good sense to be a graduate of Princeton University, where I was teaching, and that is one reason why I was eventually able to get the job working for his boss, President Truman.

It was down in Key West where Milton Kayle and I had some really interesting experiences. We were there in fall of 1951 when President Truman had Chief Justice Fred Vinson and his wife as his guests. This was one of the few times that a woman besides Mrs. Truman or Margaret was at the Little White House during the president's visits. It was during this period that President Truman had decided not to run again in 1952 and was trying to persuade Chief Justice Vinson to run for president on the Democratic ticket. This is noteworthy because, next to General George Marshall, President Truman probably admired Vinson more than any other individual.

I had never played poker prior to Chief Justice Vinson's visit. One day, the president and his aides were playing poker while I was kibitzing on the sidelines, and an amazing thing happened: Chief Justice Vinson discovered that there were five aces in the deck. Vinson was sort of a phlegmatic person and I will always remember the way he put it: "Mr. President, what would the

President Truman with Bess and Margaret on the presidential train, 2 October 1948. (TPL, 73-2808)

people of the United States of America think if they knew the president and the chief justice were playing poker with five aces? What would they think of the leadership in this country?"

Although much time was devoted to work, Key West provided a wonderful opportunity for the president to relax with his friends. The relaxed atmosphere also allowed me to get to know President Truman better. But, particularly, I had an opportunity to get to know Mrs. Truman far beyond what the newswomen in Washington thought of her. They did not like the idea that she did not hold news conferences, and they greatly underestimated her. President Truman always said at the end of a speech session, "I'll have to check this over with the Boss"; and the next day he would frequently come back with useful changes made by Mrs. Truman.

TRUMAN AND HISTORY

In his foreword, Clifton Truman Daniel made reference to President Truman's knowledge of history. This fact came home to me the day before President Truman was going to fire the most popular general in America's history, General Douglas MacArthur. The message came to me through George Elsey that I should prepare a memorandum to the president detailing the relations between Abraham Lincoln and General George McClellan during the Civil War. I did not know the purpose until I went up to the Library of Congress and began to dig around. I discovered that General McClellan looked on his commander in chief, Abraham Lincoln, as kind of a midwestern clod who did not know anything of substance about military strategy and that he—McClellan—ought to be running the war. This had a very direct similarity to MacArthur's attitude toward Truman, this World War I artillery captain of Battery D, whom he saw as a midwestern clod who did not know anything about military strategy. MacArthur thought he should be running the show—not only the military show, but also foreign policy—which disturbed our European allies. To research this memorandum, I had to hide in the stacks because the Library of Congress closed at 10 o'clock and I wasn't done. I ended up sneaking out an unlocked door of the library after midnight. I used on the cover sheet of my memorandum one of the great Lincoln stories—one he used to tell about a man who tried to get astride his obstreperous horse, but the horse put his own foot in the stirrup. The man finally said to the horse, "If you are going to get on, I am going to get off." That pretty well analogized the relationship between MacArthur and his commander in chief. At his news conference announcing the firing of General MacArthur, President Truman called attention to the precedent of Lincoln and McClellan and concluded: "The only new thing in this world is the history you have not read."

President Truman had a very interesting policy that Milton Kayle and I really appreciated. President Truman treated all the junior members of the White House staff as members of his family equal to the senior people in the administration. That is why we had opportunities such as going to Key West. President Truman also liked to have the staff come to a consensus on issues, and he allowed anyone—senior or junior—to speak up even after the consensus had been reached, right up to the final meeting on the policy. This happened at the time he relieved General MacArthur of command. When one of the junior members of Truman's staff said, "Mr. President, I think when you make your announcement on MacArthur's dismissal that you should point out that this action has the unanimous support of the Joint Chiefs of Staff." President Truman's answer was very interesting. He said, "Son, history is going to bring this out. But this is the decision of the Commander in Chief and I'm not going to pass the buck on it." You could almost hear the liberty bell ringing in the background as he made this statement. President Truman had a very sensitive appreciation not only for the principle of civilian control of the military but also for the fact that the commander in chief should not allow a general in the field to make policy.

Truman's Personality

There are other anecdotes that give an idea of Harry Truman's personality and his approach to policymaking. I heard him mention on many occasions that the rich and powerful people in this country have their own lawyers and their own accountants, their own pressure groups and their own lobbyists working for them full time. So it is the job of the president of the United States and any public official to stand up and fight for those who are otherwise unrepresented. Perhaps this view is what made Truman so admired by later generations. It has always amazed me that his stature has increased so sharply and dramatically, not because it is

Truman speaking with reporters, 16 October 1948. (TPL, 71-1217)

undeserved but because he was not so popular while he was president and when he left office. This unpopularity was primarily due to a vicious campaign by frustrated Republicans who had lost five consecutive presidential elections, the fifth being Truman's upset victory in 1948.

Executive Order 9981 is to me President Truman's most outstanding achievement. As emphasized by Michael Gardner in his book *Harry Truman and Civil Rights: Moral Courage and Political Risks,* it took tremendous moral courage and entailed political risk for Harry Truman to move forward with Executive Orders 9980 and 9981. He issued these orders in the heat of the 1948 presidential campaign, when he was threatened with defeat by representatives of the Democratic National Committee. Executive Order 9980 eliminated discrimination in federal employment and Executive Order 9981 desegregated the armed forces. Realizing that the Congress would never pass the civil rights bill he was advocating, Truman said to go ahead and used the authority of his office to do the right thing. This is, I think, the epitome of President Truman's many achievements.

As a top assistant to President Truman, George Elsey had firsthand knowledge of Truman's motivations and the specifics of numerous measures that the president took on in the face of strong political opposition. It was therefore appropriate that Elsey should write a foreword to Gardner's book on Truman's civil rights record, in which Elsey observed:

> Harry Truman's convictions, commitment, and courage are admirably recounted by Michael Gardner. He recalls long-overlooked actions taken by the Department of Justice at Truman's direction. He pointedly contrasts Truman's courage with the timidity of his two immediate successors and reminds us of the belated conversion of Lyndon Johnson to the course Truman had advocated years earlier.[1]

Hugh Sidey, former White House correspondent for *Time* magazine and currently chair and CEO of the White House Historical Association, declared:

> This is truly a remarkable book. ...Harry Truman needs to be heard today. His motto, if I may interpolate, was damn the politics, full speed ahead: do what is right. I hope that this book raises that banner for these modern poll-driven, equivocating, fund-raising, mush-mouthed, faint-hearted politicians to see.[2]

Truman was not immune to the attitudes of the times. He grew up in the rural Midwest in the late nineteenth and early twentieth centuries, and there was a section in his hometown of Independence, Missouri, that locals referred to as "Niggerneck." Some of his early letters, dating to his pre–World War I courtship of Bess Wallace, contain racial slurs. It is a wonderful mark of Truman's education and development that he was able to overcome his racist background. He even had to overcome the prejudice of his own mother, whom he revered, to be able to become the kind of advocate of justice that he embodied as president.

AN UNTOLD CHAPTER

There are so many wonderful stories to tell about Truman. There is a story about a Republican named Arthur Fleming that David McCullough omitted from his famous biography of Truman. Harry Truman was the product of one of the most corrupt political machines of this country, the Democratic Pendergast machine. He overcame this background as well, but everybody thought of Harry Truman as a bitterly partisan Democrat. His working relations with individual Republicans, however, are one of the untold chapters in Truman's political life. For example, after the Republicans had swept the midterm elections in 1946 and controlled both the House of Representatives and the Senate, Truman would only be able to get through his great monuments of foreign policy— the Truman Doctrine, Marshall Plan, NATO, and so on—with strong Republican support. All those ventures had to get through a Republican-controlled Congress, and it could only be done through the tremendous personal friendship that Truman developed with Senator Arthur H. Vandenberg of Michigan, the chairman of the Senate Foreign Relations Committee.

Arthur Fleming (later a member of President Dwight Eisenhower's cabinet) was a Republican member of the U.S. Civil Service Commission. I once asked Fleming if there was anything special he remembered about President Truman. He said that the day Truman took office a lot of the president's Democratic friends were spreading the rumor that Fleming would be the first to be fired from the Civil Service Commission because he was standing in the way of deserving Democrats receiving appointments. And so, Fleming told me, he thought the only honorable thing to do was to go to the president and submit his resignation. The minute

President Truman with his cabinet, 8 January 1948. From left: Secretary of the Interior Julius A. Krug; Secretary of Commerce W. Averill Harriman; Federal Works Administrator Philip B. Fleming; Assistant to the President John R. Steelman; Secretary of Labor Lewis B. Schwellenbach; Secretary of Agriculture Clinton P. Anderson; Postmaster General Jesse M. Donaldson; Secretary of Defense James V. Forrestal; Secretary of State George C. Marshall; President Truman; Secretary of Treasury John W. Snyder; and Attorney General Tom C. Clark. (TPL, 77-366)

Fleming walked into the Oval Office, President Truman bounded out of his chair and said, "Sit down a minute, Commissioner Fleming, I want to have a word with you. All these stories you've been seeing in the press about my firing you, well there hasn't been a damn bit of truth in any of them." And he said, "You know what? When I was a county judge with Pendergast, I didn't think very much of your goo-goo civil service. But now I'm president of the United States and I'm here to enforce the law, and you've been doing a good job, sir. You know all about this civil service merit system so I want you to stay in the job!"[3] This was all so characteristic of Truman. When a Democratic senator from Tennessee, Kenneth McKellar, wanted to get rid of David Lillienthal (Truman's appointee to the Atomic Energy Commission), Truman got the support of Republicans, especially Senator Vandenburg, to help confirm Lillienthal's appointment.[4] He could work with those on both sides of the aisle. This bipartisanship for a greater good is one of the untold stories of Truman's legacy.

In the spring of 1948, the Democrats and the Americans for Democratic Action (ADA) as well as the city bosses (Frank Hague of Jersey City, Ed Crump of Memphis, and the Kelly-Nash machine of Chicago) were going to dump Truman because they thought he did not stand a chance of getting reelected. They were going to support Dwight Eisenhower and see if they could nominate him as the Democratic candidate. Truman, it goes without saying, was upset with the ADA. When finally, in 1952, he agreed to address their annual convention, he asked some of us on the staff to get together the words of a poem by Longfellow entitled *The Children's Hour,* which began like this: "Between the dark and the daylight, / When the night is beginning to lower, / Comes a pause in the day's occupations, / That is known as the Children's Hour." Truman got up in front of the ADA and paraphrased Longfellow: "Between the Taft and the Dewey, / When defeat is beginning to lower, / Comes a pause in ADA's occupations, / That's known as the Eisenhower."

NOTES

[1] George Elsey, Foreword to Michael R. Gardiner, *Harry Truman and Civil Rights: Moral Courage and Political Risks* (Carbondale: Southern Illinois University Press, 2002).

[2] Hugh Sidney, remarks on dust jacket of Gardiner, *Harry Truman and Civil Rights.*

[3] Personal conversation with Arthur Fleming.

[4] David McCullough, *Truman* (New York: Simon & Schuster, 1992), 550.

TRUMAN, THE MAN

Milton Kayle

I am often asked how I ever came to work for President Truman. My answer is because I graduated from Hamilton College, a small liberal arts college in upstate New York, a few miles from my hometown of Utica, New York. In 1934, President Franklin Roosevelt asked Professor Henry Davenport, who served on the faculty of Hamilton College, to come to Washington to establish an organization called the National Institute of Public Affairs. It was Roosevelt's vision that the institute would offer college graduates from fifty universities and colleges throughout the country an opportunity to come to Washington for six months to experience working for the federal government. Roosevelt hoped that a number of them would eventually choose to go into public service, which actually proved to be the case. This was the grandfather of all internship programs. In fact, considering the roles that interns have played in recent administrations, the National Institute of Public Affairs probably accomplished much more than has been expected of internships!

Upon my graduation from Hamilton College in 1943, I was selected to participate in that internship program, the first Hamilton student chosen for that assignment. I had a most gratifying experience. I met Mrs. Eleanor Roosevelt and many dignitaries and eventually was assigned to the National War Labor Board. This adventure convinced me of two things: that I wanted to go to law school and that I wanted to practice law at a national level, probably in Washington.

After serving in World War II, I graduated from law school in 1948. My wife and I then made our way to Washington. Through the connections I had made with the National Institute of Public

Truman meets with congressional leaders; surrounding the president, left to right: Vice President Alben Barkley, Senate Majority Leader Ernest McFarland, House Majority Leader John W. McCormack, and Speaker of the House Sam Rayburn, 14 January 1952. (TPL, 58-10)

Affairs, I got a job first in the Bureau of the Budget in its legislative reference division and then in the Office of Defense Mobilization as assistant general counsel in charge of legislation. Both of these assignments brought me into almost daily contact with White House personnel, and that eventually led to the invitation to join the White House staff for the last two years of the Truman presidency.

MEETING TRUMAN

The first time I met President Harry Truman, I was working for Charles Murphy, who was the president's counsel, and for David Stowe, an administrative assistant whose specialty was labor matters. After I had been on the staff a few days, they brought me into the Oval Office to meet President Truman for the first time and to attend a typical conference with the president. At that time, there was a dispute between the Federal Security Agency (precursor to the Department of Health and Human Services) and the Department of Labor on a certain matter. Charlie Murphy presented the points in favor of the Labor Department's position, and David Stowe presented the Federal Security Agency's counterargument to President Truman. At that point, the president turned to me and said, "Young man, what do you think about all this?" There I was, in a room with the president, being asked for my opinion on opposing viewpoints presented by the two men for whom I worked. I was on the spot, but I was able to use sufficient circumlocution not to offend either of my bosses. However, this incident speaks volumes about President Truman. He was the president of the United States, but he took time to include me, a junior staff member, by asking for my opinion on this sensitive matter. It also reflects the confidence he had in his senior officials in their choice of staff. He relied on their judgment on personnel selection as well as on other substantive issues.

THE STEEL MILL SEIZURE

One of the most interesting experiences I had while working on the White House staff involved the seizure of the steel mills by the U.S. government in 1952 during the Korean War. At that time, a long-standing dispute between the unions and the steel industry threatened a work stoppage that could have resulted in serious shortages of ammunition, weapons, and supplies essential for our troops and for our allies in the war. Since available legislative remedies were deemed unfair or impractical and would almost guarantee a halt in production, the decision was made to seize the steel mills, based upon the inherent powers of the president under Article II of the U.S. Constitution.

It was our contention that a constitutional law issue would be avoided because the parties could be held harmless on the basis of balancing interests under equity law principles. Unfortunately, because of the way the government's attorney argued the case at the federal district court level, and the decision of Justice David Pine in that court to consider the substantive issues rather than to rely on equity principles, a constitutional law challenge resulted. On 2 June 1952, the decision came down, ruling 6 to 3 against President Truman, concluding that he had exceeded his authority as president under the circumstances at hand.

President Truman at his desk, ca. 1945. (TPL, 87-170-4)

The day after the decision was rendered, I received a call from Charlie Murphy, who said "Milt, the president is going to have dinner at Justice [Robert] Jackson's home tomorrow night, and he is going to have all the members of the Supreme Court with him. I want you to write on one sheet of paper—on one side—what was wrong with that decision." At this point, I was only four years out of law school. It would have been satisfying to work for a judge at the state or especially the federal level, or to clerk for a Supreme Court justice, and here I was with the opportunity to put words in the president's mouth, basically telling off the Supreme Court!

In my memorandum, I wrote that the Supreme Court substituted its judgment for the president's on the impact of the cessation of steel production on the military effort during the Korean War. Two biographies of President Truman record that he went to that dinner. They reported that he told the justices that he did not like their law, but that the liquor was very good.

THE LAST WHISTLE STOP

Another experience from my time working for the president further illustrates the type of man Harry Truman was. As a member of the speechwriting team, I served on the last whistle-stop train trip, which President Truman made on behalf of Adlai Stevenson's presidential campaign in 1952. On 31 October 1952, in Granite City, Illinois, Truman delivered his last whistle-stop speech, for which I wrote the first draft. The president was not at his best when reading prepared speeches; however, as was the case with whistle-stop speeches, we found that if we triple-spaced the draft to set down the basic themes, the president would extemporize by filling in the details, and this would result in a very effective presentation.

One thing I included in the first draft was the observation that had motivated the president throughout his political career, the one principle in particular: if you tell people the truth, they will do the right thing. It is a very simple concept, but so meaningful in reflecting his confidence in the American people and what democracy is all about. I asked the president to autograph the draft of that speech and he did so. The draft speech now resides in the archives of the Truman Presidential Library.

These are just a few of the stories I could tell about President Truman. It was not only a great privilege to work for President Harry Truman, but the experience was something that changed my life. He was truly a great man.

TRUMAN &
NATIONAL
SECURITY

TRUMAN AND CONTAINMENT
The Road to a Historic Legacy

John Davis

In his seminal study *The Last Years of the Monroe Doctrine,* historian Gaddis Smith remarked that after World War II critics, thinking the strategy had outlived its usefulness, suggested the United States seek a new strategic framework to supplant the outmoded doctrine. Smith noted that the Monroe Doctrine survived another four decades, enduring longer than any other such presidential doctrine, and preserving President James Monroe's distinguished legacy in foreign affairs.[1]

Following the collapse of the Soviet Union, scholars similarly argued that the doctrine of containment was antiquated and that it was the obligation of post–Cold War American presidents to search for a "new polestar," a new framework to guide U.S. foreign policy.[2] Without knowing it, these critics inadvertently began a discussion of Truman's legacy in national security. Containment is by far the most comprehensive strategy associated with any president. Variations were used through the end of the twentieth century to protect American interests. Economic containment includes legislative acts designed to unleash "economic warfare" to contain the Soviet Union, and regional plans or treaties used to stabilize western economies, limiting the threat of Soviet economic expansion.

The most salient aspect of containment, and certainly the most successful form, was found in a host of military alliances and bilateral pacts that were designed to preclude Soviet advances into fertile regions of the world. Presidential doctrines following the basic premise of the Truman Doctrine defined U.S. national security in particular areas of the world; the most significant include the Eisenhower Doctrine (1957), the Nixon Doctrine (1970), and the Reagan Doctrine (1984). In each of these areas, President Truman set the standards for how containment should be utilized. Through the containment doctrine, Truman defined postwar U.S. national security.

This paper uses two primary instruments to assess Truman's national security legacy. Richard Neustadt stated that if a presidential policy extends into multiple presidencies, or is adopted by the successor, the legacy is deemed positive. Conversely, if the incoming president discards the policy, then the policy initiative is deemed unsuccessful.[3]

More recently, Richard Haass wrote that a successful presidential foreign policy initiative is one that changes our understanding of international relations.[4] On the surface, this analytical framework seems simplistic. In reality, most foreign policy initiatives are secret, have failed, or simply were deemed insignificant and therefore did little to impart a unique understanding of international relations.

Using Neustadt's and Haass' criteria, this paper discusses why containment is a critical component of Truman's national security legacy and argues that Truman's postwar strategy outdistanced most other presidential doctrines and is equally significant for its impact on international relations.

THE STRATEGY OF CONTAINMENT

Writing anonymously as "Mr. X," George F. Kennan composed the words that defined American post–World War II foreign policy and laid the foundation for President Harry S. Truman's legacy: "It is clear that the main element of any United States policy toward [the] Soviet Union must be that of a long-term, patient but firm and vigilant containment of Russian expansionist tendencies."[5]

After World War II, perhaps the most significant issue confronting the United States involved how to deal with the Soviets. President Franklin D. Roosevelt recognized that cooperation among the great powers was vital for postwar stability, but Eastern Europe was the source of discontent among the Allies.[6] Historian J. A. Lukacs offered the classic account of this discord:

It was but the logical consequence of the division of Europe which occurred with the Western and Eastern armies meeting in the center of the continent. The tragic element here was that the Russians regarded this division as permanent and self-explanatory, whereas the Americans originally thought it to be not much more than a temporary demarcation line based on momentary military expediencies.[7]

From the perspective of the United States, the Soviet Union's overt contravention of the Yalta accords raised suspicions about its intentions and therefore threatened Roosevelt's grand design. As historian John Lewis Gaddis adds, Roosevelt indeed had a workable postwar vision, but Soviet adventurism in Eastern Europe exposed the dilemmas associated with its implementation:

> The American President and his key advisors were determined to secure the United States against whatever dangers might confront it after victory, but they lacked a clear sense of what those might be or where they might arise. Their thinking about the postwar security was, as a consequence, more general than specific.[8]

Elements within the administration began clamoring for a new get-tough approach towards the Soviet Union. Roosevelt's death did not resolve tensions among his advisors; indeed, it only exacerbated the widening gulf between factions within the administration. In the weeks after Roosevelt's death, while the new President Truman was being schooled in foreign and military affairs, confusion persisted on two fronts: the shape and direction of postwar U.S. policy, and confrontation or cooperation with the Soviet Union. This debate would be referred to as the Riga and Yalta Axioms.[9]

On 22 February 1946, Kennan forwarded the famous "Long Telegram" that settled each of the aforementioned issues and unified the new administration. In the telegram, Kennan offered the "Riga perception" of the Soviet World outlook.

> In general all Soviet efforts on unofficial international planes will be negative and destructive in character, designed to tear down sources of strength beyond reach of Soviet control. ...We have here a political force committed fanatically to the point that with us there can be no permanent *modus vivendi*, that is desirable and necessary that internal harmony of our society be disrupted,

our traditional way of life be destroyed, the international authority of our state be broken, if Soviet power is to be sure. Finally, it
is seemingly inaccessible to considerations of reality in its basic
reactions. …Objective facts about human society is not, as with
us, the measure against which outlook is constantly tested and
reformed, but a grab bag from which individual items are
selected arbitrarily and tendentiously to bolster an outlook
already preconceived.[10]

Employing the Riga analogy, the thrust of Kennan's argument
was that "ideology, and not the realities of power politics, was
the important determinant of Soviet conduct."[11]

The long telegram and subsequent "X article" became the
two pillars that formed the containment strategy. In the aggre-
gate, containment had three principle objectives: restoring the
European balance of power, reducing the Soviet's ability to
expand its influence beyond Europe, and modifying the Soviet
concept of international relations.[12] Thereafter, President Truman
embraced these objectives and they became the "cornerstone of
American postwar policy."[13]

According to Andrew Williams, "after 1947 the development
of containment based on Kennan's views, and that of 'rollback'
based on the views of Dean Acheson, Secretary of State after
1949, and Paul Nitze," ended "any residual elements of the
Rooseveltian quest for Soviet partnership in a 'one world'
NWO."[14] In other words, although Truman had fought to preserve
Roosevelt's grand design early on in his presidency, after 1947,
because of growing mistrust of the Soviets and Kennan's articulation of a postwar strategy, the president developed his own foreign policy. This policy became an important element in his
national security legacy.

President Truman had established a number of policies to
confront the postwar threat. Those initiatives included the Truman Doctrine (1947), the Marshall Plan (1948), and the formation
of NATO (1949). As significant as each of these efforts were, it
was the creation of NSC-68—a report that synthesized administration thinking on foreign and defense policy—that provided the
framework that led U.S. policy.[15] Thus, the policy of containment
provided stability within the administration, allowing a more confident Truman to instill his vision of how to confront the Soviet
Union, and stabilizing and providing direction to decision making
on matters of U.S. national security.

Discussion on board the USS Williamsburg. *From left, British Foreign Secretary Sir Anthony Eden, Secretary of State Dean Acheson; President Truman, and British Prime Minister Sir Winston Churchill, 5 January 1952. (U.S. Navy/courtesy TPL, 58-281)*

President Truman's effort to reshape and redefine U.S. foreign and defense policy could not seriously be considered or validated until the president formally implemented containment. Within the national security bureaucracy, containment would be defined through two policymaking venues: strategic planning and responding to developing crises or events. It is through these venues that the Truman national security legacy is revealed. Truman's use of containment in creating policy affected future presidents. Writing in 1986, Terry L. Deibel and John Lewis Gaddis stated that the Truman administration had used the strategic planning process in creating the NSC-68 report in 1950. Future administrations used this same process to define U.S. policy toward the Soviet Union, including President Nixon in 1969, Ford in 1976, Carter in 1977, and Reagan in 1982.[16] The Truman legacy was well under way.

THE CHANGING WORLD ORDER AND CONTAINMENT'S MULTIPLE NUANCES

From its beginning as a potent instrument in postwar foreign policy, the containment strategy had one intended target—the Soviets—but it had applications beyond the Soviet Union. The containment policy was used in the Eastern Mediterranean as a means to thwart Soviet overtures in Greece and Turkey. Specifically, following Truman's request to a joint session of the Congress on 12 March 1947 for $400 million in economic and military assistance to Greece and Turkey, a doctrine was born. In his address, Truman validated his earlier pronouncements, asserting that postwar democratic survival could only be obtained in a world free of tyranny. Thus, the United States must be:

> willing to help free peoples to maintain their institutions and their national integrity against aggressive movements that seek to impose upon them totalitarian regimes. This is no more than a frank recognition that totalitarian regimes imposed on free peoples, by direct or indirect aggression, undermine the foundations of international peace and hence the security of the U.S.[17]

After this time, Kennan's idea of containment would take on a life of its own, moving the policy far beyond the uses prescribed in either the long telegram or the X article. Noting the unlikelihood of any Soviet invasion beyond Eastern Europe, Kennan asserted that containment should consist of two components: one political and the other economic. These variants translated into the Truman Doctrine and the Marshall Plan. According to John Lewis Gaddis, these variants represented "asymmetrical containment" that "involved confronting an adversary at times and in places of one's own choosing."[18] Thus, using the containment policy, President Truman managed a host of crises, mainly centered in Europe—most notably the Berlin blockade.

After minister-level discussions over the fate of Germany broke down, and following announcement by the United States, Britain, and France of plans to convert their respective zones into one, the Soviets responded on 23 June 1948 with a devastating blockade that cut off access to Berlin. Truman feared that losing Berlin would be a prelude to losing Germany and subsequently all of Europe. Therefore, in a successful demonstration of Western resolve, Allied air forces took to the sky, flying supplies into

The lifting of the Berlin blockade by the Soviets was a reason to rejoice by airlift personnel. The airmen of Navy Squadron VR-6 greet a crew as it returns from delivering 10 tons to Tempelhof when the blockade ended, 12 May 1949. (TPL, 155)

Berlin. In the end, the American-led airlift delivered nearly three million tons of food and supplies. Stalin lifted the blockade after 231 days and 277,264 flights. President Truman's leadership during this crisis was acclaimed within the United States and in Europe.

Another component of the strategy illustrated an altogether dissimilar purpose. "Symmetrical containment" focused on two significant drawbacks to the original containment strategy: it concentrated on Europe, seeming to disregard other areas that could become sources of turmoil, and placed the United States in the untenable situation of choosing between escalation and inaction.[19]

The next crisis came in 1950 in the Korean peninsula. Records of that period indicate that the administration was considering a policy to meet regional threats. It was at this point that Paul Nitze completed the NSC-68 policy paper warning of a communist expansion beyond Europe and issued this significant statement about the invariable consequences: "The issues that face us are momentous, involving the fulfillment or destruction not only of this Republic but of civilization itself."[20] President Truman endeavored to illustrate the flexibility of containment in a region not considered by the doctrine's founder (Kennan). After North Korea invaded South Korea, Truman became convinced that the recommendations in NSC-68 should be implemented. On 30 September 1950, Truman approved a strategy that included plans to bolster the U.S. military's conventional capabilities, to strengthen its strategic nuclear forces, and to assist its European allies in improving their deterrent military positions.[21] In the final analysis, Korea emerged as a major test of the viability of containment.

Both Truman and his successor, President Dwight D. Eisenhower, were forced into situations whereby the U.S. military had to contain China on two separate fronts. The first situation developed after the People's Republic of China decided to send "volunteers" to assist North Korean forces, forcing Truman and Eisenhower to contend with a threat beyond Europe. The second

President with advisors after returning from Wake Island Conference, 18 October 1950. From left to right: Special Assistant W. Averill Harriman, Defense Secretary George C. Marshall, President Truman, Secretary of State Dean Acheson, Ambassador Philip Jessup, Treasury Secretary John Snyder, Army Secretary Frank Pace, and General Omar Bradley. (National Park Service/courtesy TPL, 65-2465)

issue involved China's actions in the Taiwan Straits. In the summer of 1954, Mao Tse-tung ordered the military to shell the islands of Quemoy and Matsu. The United States came to the assistance of the Chinese Nationalists on the islands, signing the Mutual Defense Treaty on 2 December 1954. As a result, China was forced to back down.[22]

In incidents involving China, President Eisenhower was willing to employ the most frightening and dangerous element of NSC-68—the nuclear option—to achieve desired political and military objectives. When Truman signed the directive in 1950, few thought nuclear weapons would ever be used, but in dealing with China, the nuclear option was indeed in play. A nuclear cruiser was deployed to the western Pacific six times in the next six years in response to threats from communist China.[23] This use of the U.S. Navy in Asia illustrates symmetrical containment and the dangers that accompanied it.

President Eisenhower confronted the continuing dilemma of paying the costs associated with containment. He understood and agreed with Nitze's assessment of the Soviet global threat, but was not predisposed to accept Nitze's prescription calling for major increases in defense spending to confront the threat in the Pacific. Therefore, Eisenhower and Secretary of State John Foster Dulles intended to make containment work "more effectively at less cost: the result was the first real integration of nuclear weapons in the strategy of containment."[24]

Eisenhower's successful use of containment validates Truman's containment policy. Using Neustadt's criteria that a policy is deemed positive if it is adopted by a successor, the containment policy was clearly an effective policy and an important legacy of President Truman. Eisenhower was the first of ten U.S. presidents to recognize the usefulness of the containment strategy.

CONTAINMENT AND THE BALANCE OF TERROR

From its genesis, the major problem with the containment strategy was that it included no specific military doctrine. Thus, beginning with Truman, American military policy was ad hoc, reactive, and not tied to any direct military strategy to confront the expansionist Soviet Union or its proxies around the world. Though dangerous and highly problematic, linking nuclear deterrence with containment was a novel idea. This linkage emerged under Truman (during the Korean conflict), but it was during the Eisenhower administration that the balance of terror would assume greater importance. For Eisenhower and Dulles, the United States required another option—a strategy that would alert the Soviets and the Chinese that communist adventurism into Western Europe or elsewhere would not be tolerated. In announcing the doctrine of "massive retaliation," the president had hoped to deter a global communist advance. In 1952, Dulles noted, "Local defenses must be reinforced by the further deterrent of massive retaliatory power. …The way to deter aggression is for the free community to be willing and able to respond vigorously at places and with means of its own choosing."[25]

To buttress this doctrine, Eisenhower considered the idea of preventive war. In a letter to Dulles in September 1953, Eisenhower stated,

> We would have to be constantly ready…to inflict greater loss upon the enemy than he could reasonably hope to inflict upon us. …In such circumstances, we would be forced to consider whether or not our duty to future generations did not require us to *initiate* war at the most propitious moment that we could designate.[26]

This military adjustment to the communist threat represented a tactical shift in two areas. First, the administration understood the conventional weapons option was not a sufficient deterrent to prevent war. Thus, the supplement of nuclear weapons would add an additional shock option. Second, the new doctrine embodied a movement that shifted away from symmetrical containment and back to asymmetrical containment. Finally, this all-or-nothing strategy not only alarmed the Communists but also had a major impact on subsequent U.S. presidents.

For President John F. Kennedy, containment may have been a more feasible strategy, but the reliance on massive retaliation was too problematic to implement. How, concluded Kennedy, could the United States justify the possible destruction of the world when America itself was not attacked? For both Kennedy and his successor, Lyndon B. Johnson, the strategy of "flexible response" represented a welcome alternative to massive retaliation. The strategy consisted of increasing conventional and nonconventional military capabilities, building up strategic missiles, and working to strengthen alliances and develop other non-military tools.[27]

In Kennedy's version of the New Look containment, the U.S. military would utilize the development, and eventually the deployment, of battlefield nuclear weapons to reshape American military policy against the Soviets and other communist states. Kennedy provided other objectives of flexible response in a message to Congress in March 1961:

> To deter all wars; general or limited, nuclear or conventional, large or small—to convince all potential aggressors that any attack would be futile—to provide backing for diplomatic settlement of disputes—to insure the adequacy of our bargaining power for an end to the arms race.[28]

Therefore, Kennedy's flexible response (and the accompanying idealism) expanded the options available to react to a variety of threats in a proportionate and appropriate manner and represented a return to symmetrical containment.[29] Walt Rostow, President Johnson's special assistant for national security affairs, wrote on 26 March 1962:

> It should be noted that we have generally been at a disadvantage in crises, since the Communists command a more flexible set of tools for imposing strain on the Free World—and a greater freedom to use them—than we normally command. We are often caught in circumstances where our only available riposte is so disproportionate to the immediate provocation that its use risks unwanted escalation or serious political costs to the free community. This asymmetry makes it attractive for Communists to apply limited debilitating pressures upon us in situations where we find it difficult to impose on them an equivalent price for their intrusions. We must seek, therefore, to expand our arsenal of limited overt and covert countermeasures if we are in fact to make crisis-mongering, deeply built into Communist ideology and working habits, an unprofitable occupation.[30]

During the Cuban missile crisis, President Kennedy was faced with the possibility of using the nuclear option, but instead selected a blockade to demonstrate U.S. resolve to the Soviets. Even when the tension between the two superpowers flared over the downing of a U-2 spy plane over Cuba, Kennedy refrained from exercising the nuclear option.[31]

President Ronald Reagan with Mikhail Gorbachev in the Red Square during the Moscow Summit, 5 December 1988. (courtesy Ronald Reagan Library, C47345-10)

DEATH AND REVIVAL—REAGAN AND THE POST–COLD WAR AND POST–9/11 WORLDS

Postwar U.S. presidents from Eisenhower to Carter employed containment in one form or another as the principle national security framework to guide American foreign policy. Though each president used this strategy to contain the Soviets, no president met all of the objectives associated with the doctrine. For many, containing the Soviets was problematic enough, but Kennan's stated objectives required actual implementation of a policy directed at restoring the balance power, halting Moscow's export of its revolution, and modifying the Soviet concept of international relations. No U.S. president publicly embraced these objectives; every president after Truman accepted the concept of "peaceful coexistence." That would all change during the Reagan administration.

Beginning with an address to students at Notre Dame University in May 1981, President Ronald Reagan informed the American people and the world about his administration's intentions towards the Soviet Union: "The West will not contain communism, it will transcend communism. We will not bother to denounce it; we'll dismiss it as a sad, bizarre chapter in human history whose last pages are even now being written."[32]

Many historians and political scientists dismissed this speech as amorphous and dangerous rhetoric. Upon reflection, the speech was historic: it marked the first time that a U.S. president publicly announced the goal to "transcend" communism. The question was *how*: what instruments would be employed to reach the stated goal?

To assist in the transformation of the Soviet Union, Reagan authorized a trillion dollar defense buildup that shifted the debate from "strategic parity" to a discourse on a relative qualitative (technological) advantage. Second, consistent with his predecessors, Reagan issued a strategic doctrine. The new doctrine was very dissimilar from previous strategies. Earlier presidential doctrines defined U.S. interests in a particular region of the world and warned the Soviets of consequences. The Reagan Doctrine sought to raise the costs of maintaining the Soviet empire. This was accomplished by supporting and directly assisting what Reagan dubbed "freedom fighters"—active agents to end and eventually turn the tide in what was considered the second Cold War.[33]

Third, there were critical elements that came in the form of a "silent campaign." Then secretary of defense Casper Weinberger acknowledged this: "We adopted a comprehensive strategy that included economic warfare, to attack Soviet weaknesses. It was a silent campaign, working through allies using other measures."[34]

To achieve his goal, President Reagan radically altered containment. The changes were not, however, like those of previous presidents, whose alterations were largely symbolic or cosmetic. Initially, the first change concerned the introduction of a host of top secret national security decision directives (NSDD). In March 1982, President Reagan signed into law NSDD-32, which stated that "the United States would seek to 'neutralize' Soviet control over Eastern Europe and authorized the use of covert action and other means to support anti-Soviet groups in the region."[35]

Three months later, Reagan signed a national security decision memorandum (NSDM) that illustrated the role of containment in administration policy. According to former national security advisor William Clark, "The NSDM purposefully reflected the president's strategic view that trade and finance should emerge as new priorities in our broader effort to contain and roll back Soviet operations worldwide."[36]

Though other directives were issued—NSDD-66, for example, whose objective was to actively "disrupt the Soviet economy"— none were as important as NSDD-75 and NSDD-166. A clear break from U.S. policy, NSDD-75 defined the administration's "strategy, goals, and objectives" that targeted the Soviets and their allies. In the words of the principle author of the document, Richard Pipes, "Our goal was no longer to coexist with the Soviet Union but to change the Soviet system. At its root was the belief that we had it in our power to alter the Soviet system through the use of external pressure."[37]

According to historian Peter Schweizer, NSDD-166 was an equally significant measure. The directive articulated "for the first time specific objectives with regard to the Afghan war and put them in a strategic context." The time had arrived for the administration to step up the pressure, asserted National Security Advisor Robert McFarlane: "We felt that we had created a stalemate [in Afghanistan]. If we could defeat the new challenge and up our support [more money to *mujahideen*], we could win."[38] McFarlane was arguing that NSDD-166 could force a Soviet withdrawal from Afghanistan. History indicates that the directive induced a chain reaction: first in Afghanistan, then in Eastern Europe, and by 1991, in the Soviet Union itself.

By the close of the Reagan era, and continuing into the George H. W. Bush administration, two debates assumed center stage: who won the Cold War? and, is the containment policy dead? Reagan intended from the start of his administration that the Soviet Union would end up on the "ash heap of history." By contrast, Soviet leader Mikhail Gorbachev simply wanted reform through glasnost and perestroika, not the end of the Soviet Union. In this regard, Reagan succeeded and Gorbachev failed.

President Reagan was the first to achieve all of the objectives associated with containment. In a sense, the fall of the Soviet

Union merely confirmed the legacy of Truman. President Truman embraced and implemented the novel idea of containment. President Reagan changed the parameters of the ideological conflict and redefined containment: it was no longer viewed as a strategy for coexistence with the Soviets, but as one articulated to destroy the Soviet Union.

After the fall of the Soviet Union, many scholars were talking about the "last years of containment." This debate was a product of Reagan's policies, but it also said much about Truman's effect on postwar national security policy. If the era of containment was over, Truman's legacy and influence over U.S. foreign policy had itself come to end. But during the administration of George H. W. Bush, the defeat of Iraq in Operation Desert Storm marked the revival of containment. Not only did the administration debate the containment of Saddam Hussein, but also President Bush provided yet another variation: dual containment. No longer concerned about the Soviet threat to western oil interests in the Middle East, the Bush administration warned that Iran and Iraq were the chief threats to peace in the region.[39] This policy was continued under Bush's successor, President Clinton. In the post–Cold War world, containment was granted a new mission: to contain rogue states. Truman's containment doctrine continued to influence national security policy and foreign policy.

Just as containment began to redefine post–Cold War U.S. policy, the terrorist attacks of 11 September 2001 changed international relations forever. Scholars quickly asserted that, in the post-9/11 world, America needs a new polestar to confront the latest threat to international security, the transnational empire known as Al Qaeda. In a press conference with England's Tony Blair on 31 January 2003, President George W. Bush went a step further, formally announcing the end of containment:

> After September the 11th the doctrine of containment just doesn't hold any water as far as I'm concerned. I've told you the strategic vision of our country shifted dramatically, and it shifted because we now recognize that oceans no longer protect us, that we're vulnerable to attack.[40]

In less than a month, a senior diplomat undercut the president's "containment eulogy," arguing that the administration would have to contain North Korea—a member of President Bush's declared "axis of evil"—to prevent the export to terrorists of technology related to weapons of mass destruction. This new role for containment means that Truman's national security legacy lives on.

———————————————

There are two main criticisms of Truman's containment policy and its use. Historian and columnist Walter Lippman lamented that containment surrendered the initiative to the Soviets. By implication, Truman's embrace of this strategy, according to Lippman, forever placed the United States in a reactive mode. This was illustrated in the Korean War and Soviet-sponsored wars of national liberation throughout the periphery.

George Kennan maintained that the Vietnam conflict represented a salient misapplication of containment. Moreover, containment did not imply the incessant application of military power as an active or constant instrument of U.S. statecraft. In 1967, Kennan wrote,

> I naturally went to great lengths to disclaim the view, imputed to me by implication…that containment was a matter of stationing military forces around the Soviet borders and preventing any outbreak of Soviet military aggressiveness. I protested…against the implication that the Russians were aspiring to invade other areas and that the task of American policy was to prevent them from doing so.[41]

At the time of these criticisms, both were relevant and indicative of significant problems with containment. Nonetheless, in examining the strategy as a whole and its importance in fleshing out Truman's national security legacy, both points demonstrate that no foreign policy strategy is without flaws. Containment is consistent with America's foreign policy traditions: historically most U.S. national security frameworks were defensive and emerged as a means to confront a threat to American security. Hence, Lippman's comments also manifest one sign of the times: a desire by forces within and outside government circles to confront the Soviet threat head on.

Kennan's point regarding Vietnam illustrates a recurring theme, and certainly a point for all U.S. presidents to consider: the use of force is not appropriate in every situation. In stating that the Soviets did not want to invade anyone, Kennan forgot about the 1968 Prague Spring incident, nor could he or anyone else anticipate the Soviet invasion of Afghanistan. Additionally, the Soviets employed their proxies to provide regional instability, forcing successive U.S. administrations to confront perceived threats. Historian John E. Endicott states that Russia exerted its authority in Czechoslovakia "under the guise of the Brezhnev Doctrine." Since that time, Russian forces have been active on the border with China and in Afghanistan and their surrogates have been active in Asia, the Middle East, Africa, and South America. While the Soviet Union has used its military power to challenge the United States in countries throughout the world, the U.S. has responded by maintaining its policy of "flexible containment, and doing so successfully."[42]

Using Neustadt's criteria for evaluating the success of a presidential policy, Truman's containment policy can be judged a success. Every U.S. president from Eisenhower onward utilized containment, including a reluctant George W. Bush. More telling is the fact that several presidents attempted to move away from containment (Eisenhower, Carter, and George W. Bush), thereby making a statement in opposition to Truman's policies; each, however, returned to the strategy, albeit with refinements.

For only two U.S. presidents can it be claimed that their policies had an enduring effect on U.S. foreign policy: President James Monroe (Monroe Doctrine) and President Woodrow Wilson (Wilsonian Idealism). While the policies of both these presidents left an indelible mark on U.S. external affairs, containment guided the country through more critical crises than either the Monroe Doctrine or Wilsonian Idealism.

Using Haass's formula to evaluate Truman's national security legacy—whether the policy achieved its stated objectives, and whether it changed the way people perceive international relations—Truman's containment policy would again be deemed a success. Truman achieved his stated objectives under the most difficult of conditions. As a new and inexperienced president, he transformed U.S. foreign policy through the announcement of a fundamental objective: to contain the Soviet Union. Second, in the battle to retain stability in the eastern Mediterranean region, Truman issued the containment doctrine and preserved the freedom of Greece and Turkey. Third, with the sudden outbreak of hostilities in the Korean Peninsula, Truman was presented with a choice: escalation or communist expansion. Opting for escalation, Truman used a UN mandate to contain the North Korean attempt to disrupt the carefully orchestrated regional balance. Finally, the institution of the Marshall Plan and NATO were critical efforts to contain the Soviet advance on the European continent.

In addressing Haass's second criteria, there is little doubt that containment changed the way Americans and the international community perceived international relations. From the start of the Cold War, the global community defined the Soviet threat as expansion and the U.S. response to that threat was containment. This is the brilliance of containment. Of the national security strategies put forth by any U.S. president, which one most informed the world about U.S. intentions and had an enduring impact on international relations? The answer is containment. This, in and of itself, represents an instructive illustration of Truman's legacy. But there is more.

As the central feature of Truman's legacy, containment is part of a recurring debate. The same question is asked over and over again: who is responsible for ending the Cold War, Reagan or Gorbachev? The real answer is Harry Truman. Why? Because containment prevented a Soviet global advancement, preserved the balance of power, and acted as a framework that guided U.S. foreign policy through a host of crises long before the arrival of Reagan or Gorbachev. Moreover, as great as Reagan's stewardship was in the twilight of the Cold War, his polices simply affirmed the virtues of containment. President Truman had the courage to embrace an original idea from an obscure foreign service officer, George Kennan, and that idea changed U.S. foreign policy and international relations forever. As history records Truman's legacy in national security affairs, the words that should be inscribed in scholarly books are these: "We may never again witness a more productive strategy than containment."

NOTES

[1] Gaddis Smith, *The Last Years of the Monroe Doctrine* (New York: Hill & Wang, 1994), 3–20.

[2] Graham T. Allison and Gregory F. Treverton, eds., *Rethinking America's Security: Beyond Cold War to a New World Order* (New York; W. W. Norton, 1992), 386–406.

[3] Richard Neustadt, *Presidential Power and the Modern Presidents: The Politics of Leadership from Roosevelt to Reagan* (New York: Free Press, 1990), 7.

[4]Richard Haass, "Squandered Presidency: Demanding More From the Commander-in-Chief," *Foreign Affairs* (May/June 2000): 136–40.

[5]George F. Kennan [Mr. X, pseud.], "The Sources of Soviet Conduct," *Foreign Affairs* (July 1947): 575.

[6]Andrew Williams, *Failed Imaginations: New World Orders of the Twentieth Century* (New York: Manchester University Press, 1998), 168.

[7]J. A. Lukacs, *History of the Cold War* (Garden City, NY: Anchor Books, 1969), 27–28.

[8]John Lewis Gaddis, *We Now Know: Rethinking Cold War History* (New York: Oxford University Press, 1997), 12.

[9]Melvin P. Leffler, *A Preponderance of Power: National Security, the Truman Administration, and the Cold War* (Stanford: Stanford University Press, 1992), 19–21. See also Daniel Yergin, *Shattered Peace: The Origins of the Cold War and the National Security State* (Boston: Little, Brown, 1977).

[10]Kenneth M. Jensen, ed., *Origins of the Cold War: The Novikov, Kennan, and Robert's "Long Telegrams of 1946"* (Washington DC: U.S. Institute of Peace Press, 1993), 17–32.

[11]See James McCormick, *American Foreign Policy and Process,* 3rd ed. (Itasca, IL: F. E. Peacock, 1998), 46.

[12]See "Containment, Cold War, Nuclear Policy," www.nuclearfiles. org/kinuclearweapons/strat_containment. html, accessed 31 May 2005.

[13]Charles Kegley, Eugene R. Wittkopf, and James Scott, *American Foreign Policy,* 6th ed. (Belmont, CA: Wadsworth, 2003), 47.

[14]Williams, *Failed Imagination,* 169.

[15]S. Nelson Drew, ed., *NSC-68: Forging the Strategy of Containment* (Washington DC: National Defense University Press, 1996), 3.

[16]Terry L. Deibel and John Lewis Gaddis, *Containment: Concept and Policy* (Washington DC: National Defense University Press, 1986), 118.

[17]Special Message to the Congress on Greece and Turkey: The Truman Doctrine, 12 March 1947. In *Public Papers of the Presidents of the United States: Harry S. Truman, 1947* (Washington DC: Government Printing Office, 1963), 178.

[18]John Lewis Gaddis, "National Security: Strategies of Containment, Past and Future," *Hoover Digest* (Spring 2001); and online at www.hooverdigest.org/012/gaddis.html., accessed 7 June 2005.

[19]Ibid.

[20]A Report to the President Pursuant to the President's Directive of January 31, 1950 [NSC-68], 7 April 1950. In *Foreign Relations of the United States, 1950.* Vol. 1, *National Security Affairs; Foreign Economic Policy* (Washington DC: Government Printing Office, 1977), 238.

[21]Drew, *NSC-68,* 15.

[22]Hook and Spanier, *American Foreign Policy,* 76–78.

[23]David K. Stumpf, *Regulus: The Forgotten Weapon* (Paducah, KY: Turner, 1996), 100.

[24]Deibel and Gaddis, *Containment,* 12.

[25]John Foster Dulles, Speech to the Council on Foreign Relations, 12 January 1954, *Department of State Bulletin* 30 (25 January 1954): 108.

[26]Eisenhower to Dulles, 8 September 1953, as quoted in Gaddis, *Strateiges of Containment*, 149.

[27]Gaddis, *Strategies of Containment*, 215.

[28]John J. Kennedy, "Special Message to the Congress on the Defense Budget, 28 March 1961," in *The Public Papers of the Presidents of the United States: John F. Kennedy, 1961* (Washington DC: Government Printing Office, 1962), 230.

[29]Gaddis, *Strategies of Containment*, 214.

[30]Rostow draft, Basic National Security Policy, 26 March 1962, as quoted in Gaddis, *Strategies of Containment*, 214.

[31]Graham T. Allison, *Essence of Decision: Explaining the Cuban Missile Crisis* (Boston: Little, Brown, 1971), 2–7.

[32]This transformation included not only the Soviets but also Iran. In the early months of the administration, Reagan declared a need to contain the Shia revolution. Robert Litwak, *Rogue States and U.S. Foreign Policy: Containment After the Cold War* (Washington DC: Woodrow Wilson Center Press, 2000), 158–63.

[33]Kenneth A. Oye, Robert J. Lieber, and Donald Rothchild, eds., *Eagle Resurgent? The Reagan Era in American Foreign Policy* (Boston: Little, Brown, 1987), 26–27.

[34]Peter Schweizer, *Victory: The Reagan's Administration's Secret Strategy that Hastened the Collapse of the Soviet Union* (New York: Atlantic Monthly Press, 1994), xv.

[35]Schweizer, *Victory*, xvi. A sanitized copy of NSDD-32 is available at www.fas.org/irp/offdocs/nsdd/nsdd-032.htm, accessed 3 June 2005.

[36]Ibid., 82.

[37]Ibid., 130.

[38]Ibid., 213.

[39]Robert Litwak, *Rogue States and U.S. Foreign Policy: Containment After the Cold War* (Washington DC: Woodrow Wilson Center Press, 2000), 123–57.

[40]"Threats and Responses: Facing 'Common Enemy,' Terrorism and Weapons of Mass Destruction" (transcript of news conference by President Bush and British Prime Minister Tony Blair, White House, 31 January 2003). *New York Times*, 1 February 2003.

[41]George Kennan, *Memoirs* (Boston: Little, Brown, 1967), 361.

[42]Deibel and Gaddis, *Containment*, 241.

STRAINED ECHOES OF HARRY S. TRUMAN AND THE MARSHALL PLAN

George W. Bush and the Reconstruction of Iraq

Douglas M. Brattebo

In the fifty years since Harry S. Truman's presidency, both schol-arly and popular opinion has rightly come to proclaim him a great president. The ascendance of Truman's legacy has been the result of growing appreciation for his personal characteristics and the remarkable leadership he gave the country in equally remark-able times. Of all Truman's presidential accomplishments, none has gained more luster with the passing years than the Marshall Plan. Europe's post–World War II devastation provided an open-ing for a national policy initiative of unrivaled vision, generosity, and national self-preservation that answered Western Europe's requirements for survival even as it met the needs of domestic politics. The Marshall Plan blunted what some perceived to be the very hard initial edge of the Truman Doctrine, putting in place a more measured and balanced policy of containment toward the Soviet Union. Truman made sure that the Marshall Plan was proclaimed by the right man, composed in large mea-sure by Western Europeans themselves, and promoted by a blend of justifications to fit prevailing political realities.

Over the four years of its implementation (1948–52), the Mar-shall Plan not only restored Western Europe but also helped cata-pult the United States to global primacy. Perhaps it is not surprising, then, that in the spring of 2003, as American and British troops occupied Iraq during Operation Iraqi Freedom, politicians and observers hearkened back to the Marshall Plan when contemplating the reconstruction of Iraq. What has been lacking, however, in these historical comparisons is a full appreciation of the unique circumstances that enabled the Marshall Plan to succeed. Recognizing the true complexity of the Marshall Plan illustrates just how wise and rare a leader Truman really was.

THE MARSHALL PLAN IN MEMORY

The Marshall Plan has become in recent decades the exemplar of wise post–World War II foreign policy. The words "Marshall Plan" have become shorthand for the successful provision of foreign aid by the United States and, in some quarters, the very definition of morality in foreign policy. The Marshall Plan marked the first time that the United States gave significant financial aid in peacetime to achieve its foreign policy objectives. Accordingly, one of the Marshall Plan's many enduring effects was to add foreign aid to the list of options available to national policymakers. Citizens and scholars often cite the Marshall Plan as a policy initiative steeped in altruism and humanitarianism, forgetting that it was anchored every bit as much in economic self-interest and national security. The Marshall Plan's singular standing a half century after its implementation is an eloquent reminder that national self-interest and morality in foreign policy need not repel one another. The Marshall Plan helped Western Europeans reassume control of their own destinies, but it also ushered in the era of American hegemony—a very benign and constructive hegemony by historical standards.[1]

Europe might have recovered from the aftermath of the Second World War on its own, but the process likely would have been slow and very near to disaster. Rather than hanging the prospects of the postwar order on such slim hopes of unassisted Western European recovery, President Truman and his administration had the foresight to recognize and embrace the great challenge and opportunity that presented itself. Truman's advisor Clark Clifford recalled in the 1980s that there were numerous reasons why scholar and historian Arnold Toynbee had concluded that the Marshall Plan would be regarded as one of the signal accomplishments of the twentieth century. Clifford also believed that the Marshall Plan was one reason why Truman's stock rose steadily with the public and intellectuals in subsequent years: it was emblematic of Truman's own "reputation for decisiveness, for simplicity, for honesty and for effectiveness."[2]

THE MARSHALL PLAN AND TRUMAN'S LEADERSHIP STYLE

Harry Truman deserves a great deal of credit for the Marshall Plan, but not in the way most people think. The Marshall Plan was not a presidential creation writ large, and Truman was not its sole champion. The president was savvy enough to sense that high-profile, full-bore presidential leadership was not the right approach for the situation—that something subtler was in order. Truman wisely did not place himself at the nexus of the composition, promotion, and lobbying efforts concerning the Marshall Plan. What the president did do masterfully was to blend and harmonize the ideas, demands, and concerns of interested parties on both sides of the Atlantic, in both the executive and legislative branches, and in both political parties. Truman knew what others might not have known: that he could best move the Marshall Plan forward by not constantly occupying center stage.[3]

Truman understood viscerally that his country, at its moment of maximum power and reach, must be magnanimous in victory because, as he stated in his post-presidential years, "You can't be vindictive after a war. You have to be generous. You have to help people get back on their feet." In the president's estimation, Western Europe "had to be rehabilitated by the people who had helped destroy it." What mattered to Truman, then, was that the Marshall Plan be created, enacted, and implemented, and he was self-aware enough to know that he could best ensure this outcome by orchestrating the insights and efforts of others. This clarity enabled Truman to move forward in pursuit of the desired outcome, demonstrating his talent for unadorned and, when necessary, unobtrusive leadership in the process. As Undersecretary of State Dean Acheson later recalled, "If one makes something complex out of something simple, then one is able to delay making up one's mind. And that was something that never troubled Mr. Truman."[4] At least a dozen people contributed significantly to the creation of the Marshall Plan, which might have been labeled more accurately the Acheson-Clifford-Marshall Plan. When Truman addressed a special session of Congress in November 1947, he referred to the Marshall Plan as "the result of the combined efforts of thoughtful men on two continents." Louis J. Halle, a member of the policy planning staff that drafted the Marshall Plan, said that Truman's treatment of members of his own inner circle sprang from the president's considerable "ability to appreciate these men and to support them as they supported him."[5]

EUROPE'S POST–WORLD WAR II DEVASTATION

World War II had left Europe shattered, with much of its basic infrastructure destroyed, unexploded ordnance sprinkled liberally across the continent, and millions of its citizens sick, weak, and traumatized. There was a shortage of raw materials, outdated

Truman riding through Berlin to view the devastation, ca. July 1945. Next to Truman are Secretary of State James Byrnes and Admiral William Leahy. (U.S. Army/courtesy TPL, 64-375)

factories could not be retooled to civilian production, and many skilled workers had died in the war. Inflation was a further blow to people attempting to rebuild their lives, and the unusually hard winter of 1946/47 exacerbated their privation. Harvests were meager and soon hunger was on the march. Europe's old powers had immolated themselves, and an aura of crisis permeated the daily life of survivors. "The suicide of Europe left the world with a vast power vacuum—and without any world political system to order the relations among nations."[6]

President Truman was attuned to the intense suffering of the Europeans and the ill it portended. Years later, he recalled that by the spring of 1947, "People were starving, and they were cold because there wasn't enough coal, and tuberculosis was breaking out. There had been food riots in France and Italy, everywhere." Winston Churchill, addressing Parliament on 14 May 1947, said of Europe, "It is a rubble-heap, a charnel house, a breeding ground of pestilence and hate." To Truman, the only way out of this morass was to lead through it: "The United States had to do it, had to do it all, and the people and the Congress had to be persuaded that it was necessary."[7] The Marshall Plan offered the best solution to the problem but would require remarkable leadership from the American president. Fortunately for the world, Truman was up to the task.

CONTAINMENT AND TRUMAN'S POLITICAL SITUATION

The Democratic Party—and by extension Truman himself—had suffered a decisive defeat in the midterm elections of 1946. The Republicans picked up fifty-six seats in the House and thirteen in the Senate, turning crucial committee chairmanships over to conservative Republicans and southern Democrats. After three and one-half presidential terms out of power, the Republicans in Congress were brimming over with partisan grievances and were looking for a fight. Led by Senator Robert A. Taft of Ohio, the Republican agenda centered on rolling back the policies of the New Deal at home by controlling spending on social programs, cutting taxes, and reducing the scope and reach of government. The Republican backlash in foreign policy was no less ambitious, seeking to scale back America's commitment to internationalism, the United Nations, and foreign aid. Truman, to avoid being turned out of office in 1948, was in urgent need of a political masterstroke that would put the Democratic Party back in charge. Containment, as embodied at first in the Truman Doctrine and later in the Marshall Plan, promised to do just this. Containment could unify the Democratic Party's base factions, appeal to moderates, and undermine Republican unity by making President Truman as greatly respected throughout the world as FDR had been.[8]

Europe's torpor required an active, generous foreign policy but so, in the minds of Truman's advisors and others, did the state of the domestic economy. As the United States demobilized at the close of World War II, its economy naturally took a heavy hit. By early 1946, industrial production had fallen by nearly one-third, and the number of unemployed had more than quintupled from .5 million to 2.7 million. There was talk of unemployment tripling once more, and it increasingly appeared that Europe's economic stagnation was endangering America's economic prospects. The economy began to recover by the middle of 1946 as women and college students retreated from the workplace, but policymakers and citizens did not grasp this until after the fact. American business leaders were concerned that if Germany and the rest of Europe collapsed, they would take the United States with them.[9]

By proposing greater spending on foreign aid, containment posed a unique conundrum for the Republicans in Congress. The Republicans had long opposed high taxes, extensive spending, and budget deficits; since the Russian Revolution of 1917 they had been equally dedicated foes of international communism. By early 1947, Truman was preparing to address Congress to enunciate the doctrine of containment and to call for significant aid to Greece and Turkey, both of which reputedly were threatened by insurgency and instability. The Republicans in Congress would find it difficult to oppose foreign aid designed to thwart the designs of the Kremlin and ensure economic prosperity at home; thus they could be enticed to support the president's international agenda, the resulting expenditures notwithstanding. The president's articulation of the Truman Doctrine on 12 March 1947 cleared the air. "I believe," Truman stated, "that it must be the policy of the United States to support free peoples who are resisting attempted subjugation by armed minorities or outside pressures." The Truman Doctrine "identified America's enemy and declared America's allies, and staked Truman's claim on history."[10]

In 1947, the legislation comprising the Truman Doctrine cleared both houses of Congress by substantial margins in late

April (67 to 23 in the Senate) and early May (289 to 107 in the House). The numbers were misleading, though, because the coalition of support had been difficult to hold together, and many legislators had voted for the measure under protest. The main reason was that many members of Congress had begun to suspect—rightly—that Greece had not been teetering on the edge of chaos as the Truman administration had claimed (or at least implied). In the end, Congress went along with the legislation rather than jeopardize the administration's position, but recriminations lingered. Skepticism about the Truman Doctrine quickly arose in Europe as well. The president, in the eyes of many Europeans, had not consulted the Allies thoroughly enough about the de facto break he had made with the Soviet Union. And since the Truman Doctrine was aimed at Communists everywhere, left-wing parties in Europe did not respond positively to the slight.[11]

All of this indicated a need for the president to augment and temper the Truman Doctrine with a less confrontational and more beneficent element. What was needed was "something more in keeping with traditional American longings for peace, generosity of spirit, and the ideals of the early Republic, something more in keeping with the American character, as it was seen, just after the war, both at home and abroad." As officials in the State Department pondered how to give more form to the Truman Doctrine, they became more certain that many other countries were in need of some type of aid. The idea of American postwar charity toward wartime allies and conquered enemies, previously the province only of certain journalists and newspaper editors, was gaining a foothold among policymakers in the State Department, even if it had not yet been translated into a concrete policy.[12]

From the Truman Doctrine to the Marshall Plan

The Truman Doctrine, then, was a huge step on the road to the formulation of the Marshall Plan. The Truman Doctrine crystallized after 21 February 1957, when the British ambassador, Lord Inverchapel, delivered a policy paper to the State Department that amounted to an announcement that Britain was, of financial necessity, set to begin relinquishing its empire by phasing out economic aid and support to both Greece and Turkey. Acheson and others in the State Department had been anticipating this step for several months and were thoroughly prepared for the challenge it presented. Acheson phoned his boss, Secretary of State George C. Marshall (who was out of town), and President Truman with the news. Truman promptly met with several of his advisors, and there was general agreement that the most immediate concern was the way in which the United States would succeed Britain as the dominant world power. The policymakers who had produced the Truman Doctrine began to work, and a central theme soon emerged: "which of the two systems currently offered to the world [democracy or communism] is to survive." When Truman announced the resulting doctrine on 12 March 1947, he in effect "announced that America was henceforth a world power, that it recognized no limitations to its interests, and would protect its interests everywhere."[13] The Marshall Plan would be the next major initiative to guide the United States' global interests.

Secretary Marshall paid a visit to Moscow in April 1947 to meet with the Soviets and seek a resolution on the occupation of Germany and its future status. Soviet leader Joseph Stalin was cordial but showed no interest in substantive progress. Time, the Soviets believed, was on their side; the longer the deliberations could be stretched out, the more likely that the United Kingdom, Germany, and the whole of Europe would spiral into economic collapse. Marshall had gone to Moscow believing that the Soviets were still America's diplomatic partners, but he took Soviet stonewalling as proof that he had been wrong. When the secretary of state returned to Washington on 26 April, he was determined to press for action by his own country. Before going to Moscow, Marshall had read a memorandum by Undersecretary of State for Economic Affairs Will Clayton describing Europe's economic plight, but during stops in Paris and Berlin on trips to and from Moscow, "Marshall was stunned by what he saw and heard." The secretary of state told Truman that time was wasting, and he further informed the nation in a radio broadcast on 28 April, "The patient is sinking while the doctors deliberate." Marshall summoned George F. Kennan, head of the State Department's new policy planning staff, to his office and told him to develop a set of recommendations for rescuing Europe from its peril. The secretary of state's main advice for Kennan was to "avoid trivia." Kennan collected a group of able officials to form the policy planning staff, which proceeded to investigate many specific facets of the overall question of European relief and produce reports in the form of brief memoranda.[14]

As the policy planning staff went to work, Truman dispatched Acheson in early May to address the Delta Council, an organization of progressive farmers, at Delta State Teachers College in Cleveland, Mississippi. Truman and Acheson settled on the disintegration of Europe as the theme for that address, in order to make the public and Congress aware of the need for action. Acheson told his audience that Europe was broke and required massive and immediate help. The goal was not to make European countries dependent on American largesse, but to help them regain economic health so they could stand on their own. America's freedom and national security required this, said Acheson, "and it is our duty and privilege as human beings." Even though it was clear that Acheson was speaking for the president, his speech generated less attention than hoped, although it did make some waves in Europe. Nonetheless, what Truman thereafter would call "the prologue to the Marshall Plan" was now in place.[15]

The report of the policy planning staff, "Certain Aspects of the European Recovery Problem from the United States Standpoint," reached Secretary Marshall on 25 May 1947. The policy planning staff saw a Europe that was wrecked, exhausted, divided, and insecure. A complete European economic collapse, sending more than a ripple into the Western Hemisphere, was possible, but not likely. Of more concern was the fact that if an ongoing sense of existential crisis continued to pervade Europe, some form of totalitarianism would find it a fertile medium. In particular, the Soviet Union might take advantage of the situation. It would not be enough, however, to merely react to a perceived communist threat. Rather, aid to Europe "should be directed not to combating Communism as such but to the restoration of the economic health and vigor of European society." Clayton, back from a tour of Europe, sent Secretary Marshall another memorandum on 27 May. Clayton reported that things were worse than people realized: starvation was widespread, Europe's economy actually could collapse, and if it did the United States would feel the ramifications.[16]

The policy planning staff had produced a remarkable, synoptic product. It established the United States as the benefactor of Europe and as successor to Britain in presiding over international economic relations among the Commonwealth, or sterling bloc, countries. More importantly, the policy "was not militaristic: it aroused no dread of war, it had no sound of harshness; it was a policy of generous self-interest, one that responded to the call of duty, one that called upon Americans to give themselves once more to their deepest beliefs in liberty and justice, and to the cherished ideals of Western civilization." The question of whether the Soviet Union and its satellites would be welcome to participate in the resulting aid plan was a difficult one, but Kennan was confident that the program could be promoted as open to all nations while being "constructed in such a way that the Russians and their satellites would have to refuse." Meetings continued in the Oval Office and at the State Department with the focus on preparing the secretary of state to reveal the plan that would come to bear his name.[17]

Proclaiming the Marshall Plan

Secretary Marshall spoke at the Harvard University commencement on the steps of Memorial Church in Harvard Yard on 5 June 1947. Charles Bohlen of the policy planning staff had written Marshall's speech in two days, making good use of the staff's report. The secretary of state detailed the postwar breakdown of Europe's economy, noted the possible problems that would result abroad, and warned, "The consequences to the economy of the United States should be apparent to all." Marshall proclaimed that the United States would come to the aid of Europe, stating, "Our policy is directed not against any country or doctrine but against hunger, poverty, desperation, and chaos." The purpose of the aid would not be mere relief, but restoration of a functioning Europe, and this required Europeans themselves to formulate a single, unified proposal. Marshall pledged that the United States would be willing to help develop a plan, but added, "The initiative, I think, must come from Europe." Marshall had enunciated no plan as such, but rather a grand, daring idea that captivated the American and European publics: the United States would help reconstruct Europe if its countries' governments would unite in pursuit of the cause.[18]

Truman had decided for a number of good reasons that Marshall, whom he had appointed secretary of state in 1947, was the right person to announce the plan that ultimately would bear his name. There was no one the president respected more than Marshall. As Truman recalled in the early 1960s, "I'd say he performed more important jobs for this country than any other man I can think of, and I don't know where we'd be if we hadn't had him." Indeed, historian Charles L. Mee Jr. has described Marshall as "the perfect embodiment of that extraordinary American species: the pragmatic altruist." The president had informed Marshall about one month before the Harvard commencement address of the topic of the speech, and it was then that Truman told Marshall of his intent that the plan would go down in history as the Marshall Plan, a notion the modest Marshall resisted. Truman later recalled saying to Marshall, "'You won't have anything to do with it, but that's what will happen, and that's what I want to happen.' And I was right. It did." Truman maintained that, with the Republicans in control, any plan named after Truman would be dead on arrival in Congress, but Marshall "is completely nonpolitical, he's neither a Democrat nor a Republican. He's honored by the American people. Up on the Hill they will attach no political significance to it if General Marshall is associated with it."[19]

COMPOSING THE MARSHALL PLAN

In the legends surrounding the Marshall Plan, "seldom mentioned is the Marshall Plan as a process—a U.S. government initiative requiring aid recipients to craft a coordinated strategy to achieve agreed-to objectives in accordance with basic standards set as a condition for that assistance."[20] To this end, diplomats of sixteen European nations convened in Paris on 12 July 1947, to formulate the aid proposal that would give the Marshall Plan tangible form. For the first time, European governments looked beyond national borders to cooperate in restoring and managing the economy of the Continent. And it was at Paris that the question of Soviet participation in the Marshall Plan clarified itself, formalizing the deepening divide between Europe's eastern and western halves. When Soviet Foreign Minister Vyacheslav Molotov denounced the Marshall Plan as an American plot to extend its influence into European affairs, he signaled Stalin's decision that the Soviet Union and its Eastern European satellites would not be taking part.[21] Working visits by American diplomats, including Kennan and Clayton, helped move the conference toward a consensus by its conclusion in September.

When diplomats of the sixteen nations came to Washington later in September to explain the details of their aid proposal to members of Congress and representatives from the State Department, they found that the Marshall Plan was not well known in the United States. Americans of all regions were slow to let go of their country's isolationist traditions, and public-opinion polls indicated that "barely half the population had heard of [the Marshall Plan], and of those who had, many were opposed."[22] The State Department was worried that the European proposal was too expensive (up to $29 billion), sought too much aid in cash and not enough in American commodities, and would not be supported by the American public and Congress. Upon closer scrutiny of the proposal and discussions with its formulators, however, U.S. officials came to see that the Europeans had put great thought and care into working out the plan, including the issue of receiving aid in dollars rather than commodities. The United States imposed no ideological standards and was remarkably pragmatic about the implementation of the Marshall Plan: "Individual countries reached for the ideal of a free market economy at their own pace, taking account of their individual capabilities and the inclinations and priorities of their electorates."[23]

SELLING THE MARSHALL PLAN

Cognizant of Congress's uneasiness about having been coerced into enacting the Truman Doctrine, the Marshall Plan's advocates used every available argument to make their proposal palatable to the American public and especially to Congress. As historian David Clinton has observed, this task was made less daunting by the fact that the Marshall Plan was at once "both narrow and broad." The Marshall Plan was narrow in contrast with the Truman Doctrine, which had been inaugurated with aid to Greece and Turkey but promised American aid and activism in many places and many ways. The Marshall Plan focused squarely on Europe (a place closer to the hearts of even isolationist Americans), would last for exactly four years, conformed to a general cost estimate, and would be formulated equally by Europeans and Americans. On the other hand, the Marshall Plan was broader than the Truman Doctrine in the sense that support for it could be urged on any number of grounds. According to historian Jacob Kaplan,

It was justified as a humanitarian measure, as a device for integrating Europe, as an aid to the American economy, as a way of averting war by leaving Moscow in no doubt that the United States would not abandon Western Europe, and as the best insurance if war should come, since it would preserve the states of Western Europe as functioning entities and likely allies.[24]

Even so, the opposition was intense and determined. Truman, meeting with legislators in September 1947 to discuss an interim aid package to tide Western Europe over until the Marshall Plan could be enacted, found that his committed brand of internationalism was not gaining support on Capitol Hill. Lobbyists from the State Department discovered that legislators were not very responsive to the arguments about European integration, or even about a revitalized Europe providing a market for American goods; rather, the words that did prompt a reaction on Capitol Hill were "communist threat." A communist scare gripped Washington in late 1947 as the communist parties of Western

Truman signs the Economic Assistance Act, putting the Marshall Plan into effect.
(TPL, 64-1204)

Europe used strikes and other disruptions to make things difficult for recently elected governments. Many State Department officials understood that these communist parties, having failed to win elections outright, were spent forces casting about for some approach that would get them political traction. Yet Western European governments, particularly in Italy and France, played up the danger posed by communists because they saw it as the one certain means of gaining American aid.[25]

President Truman and his team worked the anticommunist angle effectively. Truman cited in one of his speeches the dangers of "totalitarian pressures" in Italy and France, administration officials testified in Congress about the seriousness of the situation in Europe, and Clayton published a piece in the *Saturday Evening Post* predicting communist domination of Europe in the absence of American aid. All of this effort paid off when the interim aid bill moved briskly through both houses of Congress by the end of November 1947. The administration had captured the political offensive, but the real prize—the enactment of the Marshall Plan itself—was not yet secure. To maintain the momentum, Truman had his lieutenants deliver the Marshall Plan legislation up to Capitol Hill on the same day the interim aid bill passed—a sure sign that the administration's legislative lobbying efforts were only going to intensify in the coming months.[26] No argument would be ignored:

> The Marshall Plan was, Congress was told, a means to fight communism, a way to prevent postwar American depression, a way to reduce the need for more military spending, a humanitarian act, a way to rebuild the important German economy (but only after the rest of Europe, and in a way to keep Germany from rearming), a way to establish European economic and political union, a way to restore France and Italy—to keep Communists out of their governments.[27]

From the beginning, President Truman had been frank with House Speaker Sam Rayburn about the Marshall Plan's indispensability. Meeting at the White House, Truman told Rayburn that Europe was headed for depression and starvation, and that if Europe collapsed, the result would be a second Great Depression for the United States. "And you and I have lived through one Depression," Truman concluded, "and we don't want to have to live through another one, do we, Sam?" Although the Speaker was concerned about the projected price tag of European relief, he gave the president his word: "Harry, I'll do my damnedest. It won't be easy, but you can count on me to help all I can."[28]

The crucial actor in the Senate was Senate Foreign Relations Committee Chairman Arthur Vandenberg. Like Rayburn, he understood the importance of giving legislators plenty of reasons, even amorphous ones, to vote for the Marshall Plan. In response to the concern that a phrase in the bill relating to the program's impact on the American economy was too broad, Vandenberg said, "That's perfectly all right. Just leave those words in. I can tell nineteen different senators from the floor of the Senate who are worried about something, your problem is taken care of by that clause in the bill." Vandenberg also maneuvered to prevent the administration's estimates of the Marshall Plan's total cost (as high as $17 or $18 billion) from causing dangerous sticker shock to wavering members of Congress. Vandenberg knew it was wiser to specify just $5.3 billion for the first year, and then leave the balance to be handled in declining annual increments in appropriations over the next three years. This left the legislative opposition, led by Senator Robert Taft, quibbling over the first year's aid total rather than the whole four-year sum and enabled Vandenberg to move the bill unanimously through his committee in mid-February. In late February, the Communists in Czechoslovakia caused that country's government to fall, keeping totalitarianism in place as a prod to congressional action on the Marshall Plan. Final enactment, by wide margins in both houses, came in April 1948, more than ten months after Marshall's address at Harvard.[29]

THE LEGACY OF THE MARSHALL PLAN

A host of interlocking historical, political, and economic factors made possible the recovery of postwar Europe, but the Marshall Plan was almost certainly the indispensable catalyst in that complex formula. The total financial contribution of the Marshall Plan to the European economy was just over $13 billion, but the most immediate and probably most decisive benefit of the Marshall Plan, as Kennan had predicted from the start, was psychological. The United States government had come through in the clutch, and as British Foreign Minister Ernest Bevin later noted, "We grabbed the lifeline with both hands." The Marshall Plan's economic effects were formidable, but its other effects became even

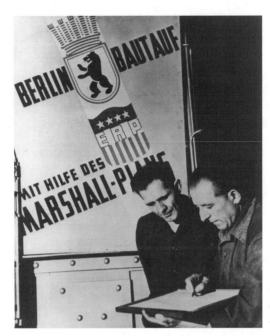

Two German workmen look over a chart. Behind them is a sign promoting the Marshall Plan, ca. 1950. (TPL, 80-21)

more impressive with the passage of time. It checked the remaining communist elements in Western European politics, strengthened centrist parties of the right and left, forced Western European governments to work together, and paved the way for European integration and the formation of lasting transatlantic ties.[30]

The Marshall Plan also played a crucial role in transforming the United States into the world's next hegemon. The formation of the North Atlantic Treaty Organization (NATO) in April 1949 followed the enactment of the Marshall Plan by one year, codifying the Atlantic community that was rising from the ashes of war. Truman had inaugurated the policy of containment with the assertive Truman Doctrine, enlarged upon it with the more generous Marshall Plan, and then institutionalized its multidimensionality through NATO. Now the United States succeeded Greece, Rome, the Netherlands, and Britain as the overseer of world order. Nearly the first half century of America's hegemony would be spent in a Cold War with the Soviet Union. The Marshall Plan reinvigorated global capitalism and set the West on a positive trajectory in comparison to its archrival.[31]

This amazing transition of the United States into the preeminent world power with a truly global reach would not have been possible without Truman's leadership or that of his predecessor, but neither could it have occurred without the painstakingly secured support of the American people. By the time the Marshall Plan was adopted, most Americans had heard of it, and despite their war-weariness and apprehension about America's assumption of the burdens of global leadership, they supported it. In both world wars, the American people had shown themselves willing to break with their country's isolationist tradition, but the question after World War II was whether support for international engagement could become more than episodic. Public support for the Marshall Plan indicated that the public could distinguish "what the United States might accomplish through economic aid from what the country could provide through military assistance or direct military involvement," thus widening the spectrum of ways for America to shape the world.[32]

THE MARSHALL PLAN AS YARDSTICK— THE RECONSTRUCTION OF IRAQ

Because the Marshall Plan succeeded so brilliantly, it "has become the yardstick with which all subsequent aid programs have been measured."[33] This has been more of a curse than a blessing. The Marshall Plan was the product and beneficiary of unparalleled geopolitical circumstances, and the types of countries it helped— industrialized powers with secular societies, functioning economies, and educated populaces—were not at all like most countries into which the United States would pump significant aid in later years. Although the framers of the Marshall Plan appreciated the uniqueness of the countries it embraced, pundits and politicians have lost sight of these idiosyncrasies and instead assumed that a Marshall Plan approach can be transferred, with equally spectacular results, to other countries at other times. Indeed, it would seem that President George W. Bush, who as a candidate "repudiated nation-building and state-building as false creeds of New Deal liberals and UN idealists, has lately become a born again reconstructionist." Bush observed at the American Enterprise Institute less than one month before Operation Iraqi Freedom commenced in March 2003, "America has made and kept this kind of commitment before—in the peace that followed a world war. After defeating enemies, we did not leave behind occupying armies, we left behind constitutions and parliaments."[34]

President Bush thus endorsed the idea that copious United States aid could do for Iraq what the Marshall Plan did for Western Europe. The best-case scenario posited was that the United States would be able to rapidly provide Iraqis with basic services (electricity, water, schools), form a functioning government cleansed of Baath Party leaders (who would face justice), use oil revenues to restore Iraq's economic infrastructure, and gradually secure the support of Iraqis.[35] This rosy view of post-Saddam Iraq, however, demonstrated several fundamental misunderstandings of the probable situation there as compared to the situation in Western Europe after World War II. First, Iraq in 2003 was almost completely unlike the nations of Western Europe in the late 1940s, for Iraq requires not only reconstruction but also nation-building of a variety that even a defeated Germany did not require. Second, aid for Iraq was formulated in a decidedly different way than aid to Western Europe under the Marshall Plan. Third, and contrary to the common belief today, the occupation of Germany was carried out in such a way that the Marshall Plan probably succeeded despite, rather than because of, the occupation's initial emphasis on widespread denazification.

At the most basic level, Iraq is a far less auspicious candidate for nation-building than was a defeated Germany. Nation-building works when the target nation has a fairly strong national identity, ethnic homogeneity, a governmental bureaucracy with true administrative capacity, previous experience with constitutional rule, and the ability to absorb significant economic assistance. Germany in the late 1940s—and Japan, for that matter—strongly exhibited all of these characteristics, whereas Iraq today exhibits none of them to the necessary degree. Iraq, with its mix of Shia Arabs, Sunni Arabs, and Kurds, is far from ethnically homogeneous. Moreover, like a number of countries in the Middle East, Iraq as a territorial entity was not created by peoples aspiring to be "Iraqis," but by the British for their own imperial purposes. Iraq's bureaucracy under Saddam became overlarge and corrupt, quite incapable of providing robust and accountable governance such as that produced by the administrative mechanisms in place in postwar Germany and Japan. Although Iraq experimented with a parliamentary system with some success under the Hashemite monarchy from 1921 to 1958, it has since become "a fractured, impoverished country, its people susceptible to hysteria and fanaticism." Thus, "Iraq's history—both under the monarchy and especially after the 1958 coup—has been filled with plenty of authoritarianism, tribalism, and ethnic and sectarian violence." Finally, as an oil state whose economy lacks diversification and synergy across sectors, Iraq lacks the indigenous capacity to absorb foreign economic assistance and utilize it effectively.[36]

These dissimilarities between postwar Germany and present day Iraq are imposing, and they become yet more significant because one of the keys to the Marshall Plan's success was that its details were painstakingly hammered out by Europeans, not by Americans. It seems improbable that the current application of reconstruction aid in Iraq could be called, at its core, an Iraqi plan. Lost are all the insights and benefits that might have been gained from bringing Iraqis together in the cause of working to compose and present a plan to serve as the starting point for rebuilding their country. Yet just such a process would have performed the same valuable function for Iraq's various factions that it did for Europeans after World War II: forcing them to think beyond their own geographical confines and other differences to seek compromises in pursuit of a democratic future.

Even charitably assessing the characteristics of Iraq as a target state for nation-building—reading its history and judging its prevailing conditions as better than those of other countries in the region, and thus believing it to have a chance of becoming a democracy—there is another problem. American policymakers have forgotten that the Marshall Plan succeeded in Germany only after the occupying forces realized that they were becoming the targets of great resentment by pursuing an aggressive brand of denazification and by pushing the values of democracy. This resentment threatened to undermine the overall effort.[37]

> In short, the real U.S. contribution was to take out the bad guys, set the ground rules for democratic reform, provide basic security—and otherwise get out of the limelight. The actual rehabilitation sprang from a combination of what General [Lucius] Clay called "the recuperative powers" of … the Germans, "Soviet frightfulness," and patience while…Germans overcame their resentment of U.S. rule and internalized their democratization in the 1950s and 1960s.[38]

The danger that occupying forces will come to be seen as too intimately involved in all the dimensions of daily life is even more pronounced in Iraq, with its long colonial history, than it was in postwar Germany. "The Iraqi body politic sees itself as having been a victim of European colonialism, and it sees the Anglo-American occupation as its second coming." Without a neighboring country for Iraqis to fear as much as Western Europeans feared the Soviet Union, and with no certainty that Iraqis possess the same recuperative powers as the Germans, one is left to hope that the United States and its allies will yet learn from the Marshall Plan and find a way to exhibit similar patience. Otherwise, as political analyst Fouad Ajami has observed, "The Arab world could whittle down, even devour, an American victory."[39]

Reflecting on the Marshall Plan in his retirement, Harry Truman told a biographer, "We always went ahead and did what had to be done, and the Marshall Plan saved Europe, and that's something I am glad I had some part in helping accomplish." A full half century later, the United States finds itself engaged in a similarly huge foreign policy effort, albeit in a different quarter of the globe and in the wake of a military campaign waged for more complicated reasons. Yet Americans and the cause of human liberty would be well served if President George W. Bush were someday, in his postpresidential years, able to make a similar statement about the reconstruction of Iraq. If such a thing is to happen, American policymakers must recall the words of General Marshall on 5 June 1947: "An essential part of any successful action on the part of the United States is an understanding of the character of the problem and the remedies to be applied." Given the potential scope of the War on Terror, there exists now more than at any time since the late 1940s the need to study the Marshall Plan, in all its complexity and uniqueness, for points of reference. In the years ahead, confronting the challenges posed by reconstruction and nation-building in various theaters, President Bush and his successors would do well to think more in terms of what needs to be done than of what will give them the greatest legacy. They must remember that history will have the final say as to whether they deserve credit or blame for particular outcomes. As Truman said of the Marshall Plan in October 1947, "I'm not doing this for credit. I am doing it because it's right, I am doing it because it's necessary to be done, if we are going to survive ourselves."[40]

Notes

[1]David Clinton, "The Marshall Plan: A Non-Presidential Consensus?" in *Foreign Policy and Domestic Consensus: The Credibility of Institutions, Policies and Leadership,* ed. Richard A. Melanson and Kenneth W. Thompson (Lanham, MD: University Press of America, 1985), 11–21; David J. Steinberg, "The Marshall Plan: Process as Prototype," in *The Marshall Plan From Those Who Made It Succeed,* ed. Constantine C. Menges (Lanham, MD: University Press of America, 1999), 249; Michael J. Baun, "The Marshall Plan: A Study of Morality and Foreign Policy," in *The Credibility of Institutions, Policies and Leadership: American Moral and Political Leadership in the World,* ed. Kenneth W. Thompson (Lanham, MD: University Press of America, 1985), 17:43–44; and Michael J. Hogan, *The Marshall Plan: America, Britain, and the Reconstruction of Western Europe, 1947–1952* (Cambridge: Cambridge University Press, 1987), 444.

[2]Imanuel Wexler, "The Marshall Plan in Economic Perspective: Goals and Accomplishments," in *The Marshall Plan: Fifty Years Later,* ed. Martin A. Schain (New York: Palgrave, 2001), 151; and Kenneth W. Thompson, ed., *Portraits of American Presidents,* vol. 2: *The Truman Presidency: Intimate Perspectives* (Lanham, MD: University Press of America, 1984), 12.

[3]Clinton, "The Marshall Plan," 21–22, 50–53.

[4]Merle Miller, *Plain Speaking: An Oral Biography of Harry S. Truman* (New York: Greenwich House, 1985), 240, 242.

[5]David McCullough, *Truman* (New York: Simon & Schuster, 1992), 564; and Clinton, "The Marshall Plan," 50.

[6]Charles L. Mee, Jr., *The Marshall Plan: The Launching of the Pax Americana* (New York: Simon & Schuster, 1984), 17–18.

[7]McCullough, *Truman,* 562; and Miller, *Plain Speaking,* 241.

[8]Mee, *Marshall Plan,* 35–36.

[9]Ibid., 76–77.

[10]Ibid., 36–37, 50.

[11]Ibid., 74–75.

[12]Ibid., 75–77.

[13]Ibid., 20–21, 36, 50.

[14]Ibid., 62–53, 88–89; and McCullough, *Truman,* 561.

[15]Mee, *Marshall Plan,* 93–96; McCullough, *Truman,* 562; and Miller, *Plain Speaking,* 244.

[16]Mee, *Marshall Plan,* 89–90; and McCullough, *Truman,* 562.

[17]Mee, *Marshall Plan,* 91–92; and McCullough, *Truman,* 562.

[18]McCullough, *Truman,* 562–63; Mee, *Marshall Plan,* 103–4; and Jacob J. Kaplan, "Never Again Another Such War," in Menges, *Marshall Plan,* 309.

[19]Miller, *Plain Speaking,* 244–45; Mee, *Marshall Plan,* 42; and Thompson, *Portraits of American Presidents, Truman,* 12.

[20]Steinberg, "The Marshall Plan," in Menges, *Marshall Plan,* 249.

[21] Mee, *Marshall Plan,* 152; Kaplan, "Never Again Another Such War," 310; and McCullough, *Truman,* 565.

[22] Mee, *Marshall Plan,* 215.

[23] Ibid., 226, 229; and Kaplan, "Never Again," in Menges, *Marshall Plan,* 311.

[24] Clinton, "The Marshall Plan," 51–53.

[25] Mee, *Marshall Plan,* 216, 230, 233–34.

[26] Ibid., 234–35.

[27] Ibid., 239.

[28] Miller, *Plain Speaking,* 246–47.

[29] Mee, *Marshall Plan,* 240–42; and McCullough, *Truman,* 583.

[30] Mee, *Marshall Plan,* 90, 259, 262–63; and McCullough, *Truman,* 563.

[31] Mee, *Marshall Plan,* 261, 263; and James E. Cronin, "The Marshall Plan and Cold War Political Discourse," in Schain, *Marshall Plan,* 290–91.

[32] Mee, *Marshall Plan,* 241; and Robert Shapiro, "The Legacy of the Marshall Plan: American Public Support for Foreign Aid," in Schain, *Marshall Plan,* 277–78.

[33] Baun, "The Marshall Plan," 58.

[34] Ibid., 58; and Douglas Porch, "Occupational Hazards: Myths of 1945 and U.S. Iraq Policy," in *National Interest* 72 (Summer 2003): 36.

[35] Porch, "Occupational Hazards," 36.

[36] Sara Kasper and Minxin Pei, "Lessons from the Past: The American Record in Nation-Building," Ciaonet.org, *Policy Briefs,* April 2003 [accessed on May 25, 2003]; Adeed Dawisha and Karen Dawisha, "How to Build a Democratic Iraq," *Foreign Affairs* 82, no. 3 (May/June 2003): 27, 48; and Porch, "Occupational Hazards," 39.

[37] Porch, "Occupational Hazards," 37–38.

[38] Ibid., 38.

[39] Ibid., 42; and Fouad Ajami, "Iraq and the Arabs' Future," *Foreign Affairs* 18, no. 1 (January/February 2003): 17.

[40] Miller, *Plain Speaking,* 245, 247; and McCullough, *Truman,* 583.

AN ENDURING LEGACY
Harry S. Truman and the Formation of NATO

Tom Lansford

Although the Cold War ended many aspects of the bipartisan consensus on U.S. foreign policy, the centrality of the North Atlantic Treaty Organization (NATO) remains an enduring component of American strategy. Indeed, in the aftermath of the 11 September 2001 attacks, NATO formed a key component of the political and military response. For instance, in 2003 NATO took over the United Nations mandate in Afghanistan, and the U.S. Senate unanimously passed a resolution calling on the administration of George W. Bush to use NATO troops in Iraq. NATO has in fact become an increasingly utilitarian organization that meets the broad needs of its member states on both sides of the Atlantic.

The first secretary general of NATO, Lord Ismay, once quipped that the alliance was formed to "keep the Russians out, the Americans in, and the Germans down."[1] In other words, NATO was created to deal with both external threats represented by Russia and internal threats represented by Germany by tying the United States into the broad framework of a transatlantic security system. During the formation of NATO, President Harry S. Truman astutely foresaw the benefits that would accrue to countries on both sides of the Atlantic. Although he faced considerable domestic opposition to participating in a peacetime military alliance, Truman realized that NATO would ameliorate security concerns of postwar democracies and affirm America's commitment to the peace and stability of Europe. Truman also perceived that NATO would bind successive administrations to this strategy.

In order to understand the true significance of Truman's role in the formation of NATO, it is necessary to probe four questions. First, what did the United States, and specifically the Truman administration, hope to gain from formal involvement in a European-based security system? Second, what did the Europeans seek to gain from the United States in the context of NATO? Third, what was Truman's role in establishing the alliance? Finally, how has the legacy of Truman been manifested within the context of NATO? Analysis of these questions demonstrates the true importance of Truman's role in creating the most successful peacetime military alliance in world history and in promoting American bipartisan consensus on foreign policy that continues today through support for NATO.

U.S. INTERESTS

The onset of the Cold War reordered the wartime alliances that had marked U.S. foreign policy under Franklin D. Roosevelt. An adroit student of history, Truman sought to avoid the mistakes made in the aftermath of World War I by preventing a return to isolationism. He also understood the ramifications of the emerging conflict with the Soviet bloc and the need to mobilize the resources of the United States. Writing in his memoirs, Truman declared:

> Never before in history has one nation faced so vast an undertaking as that confronting the United States of repairing and salvaging the victors as well as the vanquished. The complete surrender of the Axis powers did not bring any relaxation or rest for our people. They had to face and were ready to make whatever new sacrifices were necessary to insure the peace.[2]

Truman further perceived the true nature of the communist regimes. As early as 1945, he wrote that communist states were ruled by "clubs, pistols and concentration camps."[3]

In response to the need to rebuild areas of Europe and Asia, and to contain the spread of Soviet influence, the administration enacted a variety of programs, including the Marshall Plan and the Truman Doctrine. These programs highlighted the president's ideological association with "Wilsonian internationalism," but also confirmed the fact that, as historian Arnold A. Offner states,

Truman's "internationalism reflected unquestioned faith in American moral superiority."[4] The Marshall Plan and the Truman Doctrine formed the initial core of the containment doctrine that would itself serve as the foundation of U.S. foreign policy throughout the Cold War.

In order to contain Soviet expansion without dramatic increases in defense outlays, Truman ultimately sought to develop a series of regional defense agreements, especially as repeated Soviet vetoes of UN military proposals cast doubt on that institution's ability to fulfill its collective defense goals. This strategy was first manifested through the 1947 Inter-American Treaty of Reciprocal Assistance, commonly known as the Rio Pact. However, while the Rio Pact met with broad acceptance in the United States and the rest of the Western Hemisphere, the creation of NATO would face several domestic and international hurdles.[5]

CONTAINMENT

The immediate U.S. interest behind the establishment of NATO was the administration's containment policy. The policy articulated by George Kennan was first presented to the public in 1947 as an anonymous essay in the journal *Foreign Affairs*.[6] In the essay, Kennan argued that the Soviet foreign policy was marked by "secretiveness, the lack of frankness, the duplicity, the war suspiciousness, and the basic unfriendliness of purpose." Kennan contended that "these characteristics of the Soviet policy, like the postulates from which they flow, are basic to the internal nature of Soviet power, and will be with us...until the nature of Soviet power is changed." In order to force such a change on the Soviets, Kennan argued (in what became the plan for implementing the containment doctrine) that the United States

> has it in its power to increase enormously the strains under which Soviet policy must operate, to force upon the Kremlin a far greater degree of moderation and circumspection than it has had to observe in recent years, and in this way to promote tendencies which must eventually find their outlet in either the breakup or the gradual mellowing of Soviet power. For no mystical, messianic movement—and particularly not that of the Kremlin—can face frustration indefinitely without eventually

adjusting itself in one way or another to the logic of that state of affairs.[7]

Kennan's ideas would be enthusiastically embraced by senior members of the Truman administration. Future secretary of state Dean Acheson noted that this era

saw the entry of our nation, already one of the superpowers, into the near chaos of a war-torn and disintegrating world society. To the responsibilities and needs of that time the nation summoned an imaginative effort unique in history and even greater than that made in the preceding years of fighting. All who served in those years had an opportunity to give more than a sample of their best.[8]

To implement the doctrine, the Truman administration asserted that the United States "required a new degree of military vigilance and a permanent program of preparedness in which all of the nation's resources, civilian and military alike, were mobilized against a ruthless and implacable enemy." However, the administration also sought to ensure that the United States would not be directly threatened by Soviet military action.[9]

DOMESTIC CONSTRAINTS ON TRUMAN

In many ways, Truman faced his most significant opposition from domestic sources. Historian Michael Hogan contends that the isolationist wing of the Republican Party, led by figures such as Senator Robert A. Taft and former president Herbert Hoover, "were convinced that a powerful national security state would waste precious resources, regiment the nation's youth, and concentrate too much authority in the state, particularly in its military arm."[10] Taft believed that assistance to foreign states undermined the American economy by causing undue taxation and depriving the domestic economy of needed capital. Truman repeatedly faced isolationist reservations about his policies, although the attacks were more constrained they had been during Wilson's administration. Although Taft's extreme isolationism had moderated in the aftermath of World War II, he vehemently opposed NATO because he believed it committed the U.S. to an automatic defense of Europe. A broad coalition of both the political left and right resisted Truman's policies on a number of fronts, arguing that the growing militarization of U.S. foreign policy would unduly strengthen the executive branch, and that administration plans would "weaken the home, the church, and the school as counterweights to federal authority and would undermine the constitutional balance, first by creating an executive branch strong enough to overwhelm Congress and then by creating a military caste strong enough to overwhelm the president." Many in Congress felt that the United States could use sea and air power to protect itself, and any rigid foreign security commitment would place American ground troops at needless risk.[11]

Tensions between the Democrats and Republicans were heightened in the aftermath of the 1948 election. Truman's victory over Republican candidate Thomas E. Dewey, coupled with Democratic gains in the House and Senate, increased congressional partisanship since the minority status of Republicans in the Senate gave them little incentive to cooperate on foreign policy. The election losses also meant that the leadership of the Republican Party became more narrowly partisan.[12] Truman would ultimately have the lowest percentage of bipartisan support in the Senate of the Cold War presidents with the exception of Jimmy Carter and Ronald Reagan.

Table 1. Bipartisan support on defense and foreign policy voting

Administration	Percentage of support	Number of votes
Truman	53.9	41
Eisenhower	72.2	135
Kennedy	61.3	57
Johnson	72.0	167
Nixon	57.9	62
Ford	57.9	62
Carter	40.9	81
Reagan	42.1	62

Data from James Meernik, "Presidential Support in Congress: Conflict and Consensus on Foreign and Defense Policy," *Journal of Politics* 55 (Aug. 1993): 572.

The key to overcoming the Taft wing of the Republican Party was cooperation with key moderate Republican leaders such as Arthur Vandenberg. Taft and Vandenberg had a tacit arrangement whereby Taft concentrated on domestic issues and Vandenberg was considered the party leader on foreign policy. Vandenberg became the main force in securing Republican support for the Marshall Plan and the Truman Doctrine in the Senate and was particularly influential in policy debates within the Republican Policy Committee.[13] The Truman administration would work closely with Vandenberg as the negotiations over NATO began.

Administration policy was also restrained by a continuing "guns or butter" debate over the ability of the government to maintain security commitments and also guarantee the domestic economy. A compromise would prove possible only through deficit spending. Truman accepted this, as it became clear that the budget could not be balanced with both expanded military budgets and increases in social programs.[14] Truman was already committed to increased domestic spending through the Fair Deal, and he realized that one way to control the increase in military spending and still contain the Soviets was to develop military alliances.

The formal and tacit alliances that the Truman administration initiated maintained the emphasis on multilateralism in U.S. foreign policy, but they were also an attempt to promote burden sharing among the nation's closest allies.[15] Truman and his advisors understood that one way to lessen the costs of American security guarantees in Europe was to have the Europeans take on a greater share of the burden of their own defense. However, in the midst of their rebuilding efforts, European capitals were confronted with budgetary constraints, including the cost of empires, and initially showed little inclination to supplant U.S. troops and military assets because of the additional costs.

EUROPEAN INTERESTS

Central to the security policies of the Western European powers was an interest in maintaining significant U.S. conventional forces on the Continent. This was seen as the optimum guard against both Russian aggression and German resurgence. The Western democracies faced a variety of economic, political, and security problems in the immediate post–World War II era. In security terms, three main issues confronted the war-weary governments of the region: How could the Soviet military threat be countered? What should Germany's role be in Europe (even a divided and democratic West Germany)? and How could the Western European countries best maintain U.S. participation in continental security? The key to the first two dilemmas was the third. When Germany surrendered in 1945, the United States had 3.1 million troops stationed in Europe. Within a year, the figure decreased to 391,000. In addition, all 299,000 Canadian troops were withdrawn and British forces were cut from 1.3 million to 488,000. In contrast, the Soviets had some 2 million troops deployed in the region and undertook steps to begin to develop military forces within those states under Soviet hegemony. By 1948, there were only 12 understrength divisions among the Western European states, with total American ground reserves of 2½ divisions. In contrast, the Soviets had 25 divisions deployed and 140 other divisions at full battle strength.[16]

Faced with economic collapse, the major European governments perceived that the only way to counterbalance the internal and external threats was to develop collaborative defense structures and increase the American military commitment. Belgian prime minister (and future secretary general of NATO) Paul-Henri Spaak summarized the fear of the Europeans in a speech to the UN in 1948: "There is but one Great Power that emerged from the war having conquered other territories, and the Power is the USSR."[17]

COLLECTIVE SECURITY

The first major step in the formation of NATO was the establishment of an anti-German defensive agreement between Britain and France, the 1947 Dunkirk Treaty. In January 1948, British Foreign Secretary Ernest Bevin met with U.S. Secretary of State George Marshall and suggested a series of bilateral agreements to expand the Dunkirk Treaty to cover all external threats, not simply German aggression. Truman thought the idea was a "good beginning" and ordered Marshall to pledge U.S. support.[18] Bevin's original proposal for bilateral agreements was replaced when Marshall suggested the Rio Pact as a model for a collective organization. The Dunkirk Treaty was superceded in March 1948 by the

Brussels Treaty, which linked France, Great Britain, Belgium, the Netherlands, and Luxembourg in a broad defensive alliance, the Western European Union or WEU. The WEU was seen by the Europeans as a first step toward a wider transatlantic alliance that would include the United States.[19]

The British were particularly keen to tie the United States to European security for two reasons. First, the postwar government could not maintain its military deployments in Europe and simultaneously station troops in the various colonies. Second, the British were concerned that Soviet gains in Hungary, Poland, and Czechoslovakia might propel to power leftist parties in other European states, moving the Iron Curtain farther to the west.[20] Meanwhile, for the French, a U.S. troop presence provided the best means to contain Germany and Italy. Smaller European states perceived that the United States could serve as a counterweight to domination by their larger neighbors, mainly France and Great Britain.

Just after the Brussels Treaty was signed, the Berlin blockade began. The blockade heightened Western European concerns over Soviet aggression. It also reinforced perceptions about the capabilities of the United States. In April 1948, the WEU members began emergency sessions to determine defense needs and capabilities; significantly, the United States and Canada were invited to attend as observers.

BRINGING IN THE UNITED STATES

Even with the establishment of the WEU, Truman understood that more was needed to maintain peace and stability in Western Europe. The State Department warned that efforts such as the WEU would have little "practical value" unless the United States was a member.[21] Truman found potential parallels between the WEU and the failed League of Nations, and recognized the need for U.S. participation. The president's closest advisors supported his sentiments. Soon after the formation of the WEU, the National Security Council (NSC) recommended that Truman initiate talks to develop a collective defense agreement for the North Atlantic area that would be based on the Rio model but would include agreements on specific aspects of cooperation, including deployments and coordination of defense production.[22]

While the administration supported concrete defense ties with the Western Europeans, there continued to be opposition in the United States. The Taft wing of the Republican Party, and even American military officials, expressed concern that increased defense aid to the Europeans might undermine domestic efforts to augment the military. In order to lay the groundwork for what would become NATO, Truman asked Marshall and Undersecretary of State Robert M. Lovett to enter into talks with Vandenberg and Democratic Senator Tom Connally of Texas.

The result of these discussions was the Vandenberg Resolution (Senate Resolution 239). The resolution recommended "the association of the United States by constitutional process, with such regional and other collective arrangements as are based on continuous and effective self-help and mutual aid, and as affect its national security."[23] With Democratic support in the Senate assured, Vandenberg was able deliver Republican votes; the resolution passed 64 to 4 on 11 June 1948.

The Vandenberg Resolution was seen as a signal from the United States in support of a broad, multilateral transatlantic defense system. Both Canada and Great Britain publicly announced support for a collective defense agreement for the North Atlantic to supersede the WEU. On 6 July 1948, Undersecretary Lovett opened a series of discussions in Washington with his Canadian and European counterparts. The Washington negotiations ended on 9 September 1948 and produced a report that called for a transatlantic defense treaty. The report was approved by the WEU in October; in December formal negotiations began in Washington on the creation of NATO. Meanwhile, the administration also began work on a military assistance program, which served as the main conduit of U.S. arms and equipment for the European allies. Most significantly, the program was also designed to ensure interoperability between the allied forces in Western Europe by coordinating weapon and equipment types for the various national militaries.

THE FORMATION OF NATO

Although Truman regained Democratic majorities in both houses of Congress following the 1948 elections, he faced a more hostile Republican minority when the real negotiations over NATO began. Dean Acheson replaced the venerated Marshall as secretary of state, but he lacked the national prestige of his predecessor and would be called into question more frequently than Marshall had been. Nonetheless, Truman was determined to proceed. In his inaugural address, Truman announced,

> We are now working out with a number of countries a joint agreement designed to strengthen the security of the North Atlantic area. Such an agreement would take the form of a collective defense arrangement. ...The primary purpose of these agreements is to provide unmistakable proof of the joint determination of the free countries to resist armed attack from any quarter. Every country participating in these arrangements must contribute all it can to the common defense.[24]

Truman also declared that he hoped to soon send to the Senate a treaty on the proposed arrangement.

Truman demonstrated great political agility in the debate over which countries should be included in NATO. His preference was for the proposed organization to be as broad as possible. He directed the State Department to explore the inclusion of states beyond the United States, Canada, and the WEU members. It was decided that the United States would first approach the WEU states, and then approach Denmark, Iceland, Norway, Sweden, and Italy.[25]

Truman was particularly interested in ensuring that countries with strategic importance such as Norway and Iceland be included (even though it was understood that neither could contribute significant forces to a future alliance). The Vandenberg Resolution required that any future alliance be advantageous to the U.S., and Truman believed that the inclusion of these key states would help ensure ratification in the U.S. Congress. Truman also understood the importance of Italy, even though few in 1948 would consider the nation an Atlantic state. In addition to its strategic position in the Mediterranean, Italy shared a border with France, and Italian inclusion in a collective security organization would allow the French to shift forces from its border with Italy to face the Soviet threat. The president equally understood the reluctance of those nations opposed to admitting Italy. He commented in his memoirs, "One had to remember that the British had had some bad experiences with Italy in recent years." There was also concern in the U.S. about the potential for a communist takeover of Italy.[26]

Truman and officials from both the State and Defense Departments dexterously maneuvered the negotiations throughout the winter of 1948/49. Each of the European states wanted substantial military assistance[27] and also had political preferences that often ran counter to each other. For instance, the French bid to include Italy was opposed by the British government, which, as historian Antonio Varsori noted, viewed Italy as a member of "a group of second-class nations which had no right, at least for the time being, to become members of the inner circle of the Western world." The British military also strongly believed that Italy could not be defended and that inclusion of the Italians might prompt the Soviets to test the alliance. Furthermore, the members of the WEU were reluctant to endorse the membership of states such as Denmark or Norway since it was perceived that their inclusion would dilute the amount of American military aid for each individual member state. Finally, France wanted its colonies in Algeria, Tunisia, and Morocco covered by any transatlantic alliance. The French argued that they were an integral part of France; as Armand Bérard, the French representative to the Washington talks, pointed out, "How could Algeria be excluded when Alaska was included within the sphere of the application of the treaty?"[28]

THE WASHINGTON TREATY

The agreement that created NATO was the result of a series of discussions, known as the Washington Exploratory Talks on Security (or WET for short), between the United States and its main allies, including Canada and various European states from July 1948 to March 1949. Following the inauguration of the slightly new administration, Acheson took over the immediate direction of the talks. By March of 1949, agreement had been reached on the main principles of the Washington Treaty and on membership. Acheson formally announced the treaty on 18 March 1949 and stated that "the paramount purposes of this Pact are peace and security."[29]

On 4 April, the Washington Treaty was signed in the nation's capital by representatives of the twelve founding states of NATO:

President Truman signs and puts into effect the North Atlantic Treaty, 24 August 1949. From left to right: Sir Derick Hoyer Miller, Charge D'Affaires, United Kingdom; Ambassador Henrik DeKauffmann of Denmark; W. D. Matthews, Counselor of the Canadian Embassy; Secretary of Defense Louis Johnson; Ambassador Henri Bonnet of France; Ambassador Pedro Theotonio Pereira of Portugal; Secretary of State Dean Acheson; Jonkheer O. Reuchlin, Charge D'Affaires, the Netherlands; and Mario Lucielli, Counselor of the Italian Embassy. (Abbie Rowe, National Park Service/courtesy TPL, 73-3193)

the United States, Canada, Belgium, Denmark, France, Great Britain, Iceland, Italy, Luxembourg, the Netherlands, Norway, and Portugal. While the treaty called for various measures to strengthen security, the key to the Alliance was Article 5, which pledged the members to jointly respond to an attack on any single member state.[30]

NATO's FOUNDING PRINCIPLES

In his speech at the signing of the Washington Treaty, Truman stated the hope that although NATO was a security organization, its existence would reinforce the economic and political recovery of the region: "In this pact, we hope to create a shield against aggression and the fear of aggression—a bulwark which will permit us to get on with the real business of a government and society—the business of achieving a fuller and happier life for our citizens." Truman also declared, "We believe that our method of achieving international unity through the voluntary association of different countries dedicated to a common cause is the only way of bringing order to our troubled world."[31]

Truman's inaugural address had enunciated the main American interests in NATO, and his sentiments were repeated in his speech at the signing. First, NATO was to be both a defensive alliance and a collective security arrangement. Defensive alliances are designed to protect states against external threats. These arrangements tend to be short-lived, since once the threat is gone, there is no longer a need for the alliance or coalition. Meanwhile, collective security systems focus on internal threats and self-regulation. Hence, NATO was formed to counter Soviet aggression, but it also served to rehabilitate states such as Germany and Italy. Second, NATO was based on burden sharing. Under the Truman administration, the United States would commit to transatlantic security, but it would only do so with the understanding that its Canadian and European partners would also contribute significantly to regional security. Burden sharing would be formalized in the twin principles of the subsequent military assistance program, self-help and mutual aid. Finally, NATO, like the Marshall Plan, was designed to reinforce American preferences in Europe, including free trade and democracy. Through NATO, political momentum would promote and reinforce liberal democracy in Western Europe.[32]

Proponents of the treaty in the U.S. Senate, led by Vandenberg and Connally, assured Truman that the measure would face relatively little resistance in the chamber. When Truman sent the Washington Treaty to the Senate for ratification, he declared:

> Events of this century have taught us that we cannot achieve peace independently. The world has grown too small. The oceans to our east and west no longer protect us from the reach of brutality and aggression. We have also learned—learned in blood and conflict—that if we are to achieve peace we must work for peace. This knowledge has made us determined to do everything we can to insure that peace is maintained. We have not arrived at this decision lightly, or without recognition of the effort it entails. But we cannot escape the great responsibility that goes with our great stature in the world.[33]

In this message, Truman acknowledged the great step he was taking. For the first time in its history, the United States was about to join a permanent peacetime military alliance and in doing so,

Truman would violate George Washington's warning to avoid "entangling alliances." For the United States, membership in NATO set a precedent:

> For the first time in its history the country had committed itself to an alliance in peacetime. Instead of again allowing the balance of power to be upset and once more becoming drawn into a war after it started, the United States now expected to prevent this by committing itself to the preservation of the European balance of power on a permanent basis. Collective security under NATO would be combined with economic development efforts to seal the long-term cooperation of the United Sates and its allies in Western Europe.[34]

Truman's efforts to "advise" the Senate as the administration initiated the WET, together with his relationship with Vandenberg, led to relatively easy ratification of the treaty in the Senate. The Washington Treaty was submitted on 12 April 1949 and ratified on 21 July on a vote of 82 to 13 (although, as Truman was fond of pointing out, "eleven of these thirteen were Republicans"[35]).

MAKING NATO WORK

The signing of the Washington Treaty confirmed American participation in European security, although the degree of commitment was initially unclear. Truman needed to provide substantial military aid to the new member states of NATO in order for the alliance to become operational. Consequently, he asked Congress for $1.4 billion for arms and equipment for the NATO states and other important U.S. allies such as Greece and Turkey. Truman asked for the funds with the understanding that the United States was "not arming ourselves and our friends to start a fight with anybody. We are building defenses so that we won't have to fight."[36]

Truman's request became codified through the Mutual Defense Assistance Act of 1949. Truman and his senior defense planners hoped that the act would establish a rough division of labor in regards to European security. The United States would provide arms and equipment and would oversee strategic and tactical bombing and naval operations, but the Europeans would be responsible for providing the majority of conventional ground forces. Truman called on the British and French to provide the main air power.[37]

THE KOREAN WAR

The advent of the Korean War led the administration to attempt to move the defensive line in Europe as far to the east as possible. Truman was particularly concerned that the Soviets might view American preoccupation in Asia as an opportunity to initiate action in Europe. He noted that "the attack upon Korea makes it plain beyond all doubt that communism has passed beyond the use of subversion to conquer independent nations and will now use armed invasion and war."[38] The Korean War also led Truman to pressure the European allies into expanding the alliance to include Greece and Turkey, who became associate members in September 1950 and then full members in 1952.[39]

Meanwhile, there was growing pressure to integrate NATO's military forces. In 1950, NATO foreign ministers endorsed the principle of an "integrated military force adequate for the defense of freedom in Europe." War hero Dwight D. Eisenhower was chosen to be NATO's first military commander. However, the decision to integrate American forces with the European allies opened a great debate in Congress, which brought together isolationists, hawks, and "Asia-first" proponents unhappy with the Truman-Acheson foreign policy management. Congress ultimately assented to Eisenhower's appointment and to the deployment of four additional American divisions to Europe after moderate Republicans, including Senator Henry Cabot Lodge of Massachusetts and former presidential candidate Dewey, supported the measures. Truman called the Senate vote "further evidence that the country stood firm in its support of the North Atlantic Treaty." Although Congress asserted its right to approve future deployments in support of NATO, historian Gaddis Smith notes that "the Truman administration did not again suffer a formidable Congressional attack on its European objectives."[40]

The main impetus for congressional support of NATO was a growing fear on both sides of the Atlantic that the Soviets could easily overrun the outnumbered ground forces of the NATO allies. While American military planners studied the idea of a joint European command, Truman continued to press the allies to develop greater military capabilities. In response, NATO established a Defense Financial and Economic Committee and a Military Production and Supply Board to facilitate cooperation, oversee allied military production, promote standardization of military equipment and parts, and provide technical assistance with development and production of weapons. At the May 1950 meeting in London, the NATO ministers, with American prompting,

> urged their governments to concentrate on the creation of balanced collective forces in the progressive buildup of the defense of the North Atlantic area, taking at the same time fully into consideration the requirements for national forces which arise out of commitments external to the North Atlantic area.[41]

For the Truman administration, 1952 was the year of "maximum danger"—the point at which U.S. planners judged that Soviet nuclear capabilities and their conventional forces would be able to overwhelm Western Europe's defenses, even with U.S. nuclear support. The administration initiated an ambitious military buildup and began to shift the focus of American aid to Western Europe from economic to military aid.[42] In 1951, for instance, France was awarded some $600 million in economic assistance, but half of that came from funds designated under the Mutual Security Act. Concurrently, Great Britain was given $300 million to bolster defense-industrial production.

Truman was also willing to raise the number of American troops in Europe but stated, "Our plans are based on the sincere expectation that our efforts will be met with similar action on their part." He also insisted that steps be taken to incorporate West Germany into the framework of transatlantic security. In 1950, NATO pledged to "treat any attack against the Federal Republic or Berlin from any quarter as an attack upon themselves." The administration even proposed in September 1950 that Germany raise ten divisions to operate under the auspices of NATO. In his first annual report as the Supreme Allied Commander in Europe, Eisenhower concluded that "even with the maximum potential realized through collective efforts of member nations, there is little hope for the economical long-term attainment of security and stability in Europe unless Germany can be counted on the side of the free nations."[43]

Throughout Truman's presidency, France resisted efforts to rearm Germany, even in the context of NATO. Secretary of State

The official flag of the Allied Atlantic Command, NATO, April 1952. (U.S. Navy/courtesy TPL, 96-752)

Acheson warned Truman that "no French Government could face the French Assembly or French public opinion with the proposition of reestablishing at this time Germany united which might in any way build the framework of a German army."[44] Truman and American military planners wanted German participation to alleviate the need for massive numbers of U.S. ground troops; the nascent German government complicated issues by seeking extensive concessions in exchange for NATO membership. Unable to find a compromise, the European Defense Community (EDC), a French initiative, was seen as the way to incorporate Germany. The EDC was designed to be a fully integrated European army in which German forces would be under the command of other nations, thereby providing a means to "rehabilitate" West Germany. The Germans saw the EDC as the most likely way to reintegrate West Germany into the community of nations of Western Europe. German Chancellor Konrad Adenaur described the EDC as an "indispensable prerequisite for peace in Europe."[45] Although the EDC would ultimately collapse during the Eisenhower administration, it provided the framework for German rearmament and paved the way for the eventual entry of the Federal Republic into NATO in 1955.

TRUMAN'S LEGACY

When Truman left office in 1953, all of the major components of NATO were in place. He had broken the taboo against foreign alliances or "entanglements," and subsequent presidents would follow his example. The success of NATO sparked the creation of other security organizations as Eisenhower's administration sought to replicate the achievements of the transatlantic alliance during the "pactomania" of the 1950s.[46] Future presidents would never again face the same magnitude of domestic constraints on membership in international organizations.

Truman's greatest impact on the structure of NATO was his belief that the alliance should be a broad rather than a narrow organization. From the beginning he sought to expand membership beyond the United States and the WEU states. He also supported expansion of NATO to include geographic areas outside of the traditional transatlantic region. Hence, Italy, Greece, and Turkey joined NATO during Truman's tenure. By supporting NATO expansion, Truman helped export the principles of democracy and civilian control of the military, and established NATO as a key ingredient for stability throughout the greater part of Europe.

Since 1953, successive rounds of NATO expansion have brought the number of current members to nineteen, including states from the former Warsaw bloc—the Czech Republic, Poland, and Hungary. In 2002, NATO agreed on its most ambitious expansion to bring in most of the remaining Central and Eastern European states, including Bulgaria, Estonia, Latvia, Lithuania, Romania, Slovakia, and Slovenia. NATO officials have pledged that this is not the end of expansion even though the number of countries in the alliance will rise to twenty-six. As a testament to continued bipartisan support for NATO, in May 2003, the U.S. Senate voted 96 to 0 to approve the enlargement. NATO's two most recent rounds of expansion occurred under a Democratic president, Bill Clinton, and a Republican, George W. Bush—a testament to the continued bipartisan support the organization enjoys in the United States.

Organizationally, Truman moved beyond what most Americans, and indeed most Europeans, sought to accomplish through NATO. This also reflected his vision for a broad, comprehensive alliance. Initially, NATO was seen as a coordinating body for the allied forces. Yet the impetus for stronger military preparedness, brought on by the Korean War, prompted the creation of an integrated command system. Truman adroitly offered the war hero Eisenhower as the first military commander of NATO.

The effectiveness of NATO today is due in large part to the decisions to integrate the military command and therefore increase unit-to-unit contacts, training, and operational efficiency. Truman's efforts to promote European defense self-sufficiency, which led to the creation of bodies such as the Defense Production Board, helped ensure interoperability among NATO forces. It is this ability for troops from different national armies to conduct operations that has epitomized the alliance and led to the success of NATO peacekeeping missions in the Balkans and combat operations in Kosovo and Afghanistan.

NATO was formed to deal with external threats (the Soviet Union) and with internal threats (Germany), and to keep the United States engaged in European security. Truman's greatest legacy in the context of NATO is the fact that the organization continues to fulfill these three core missions. At the heart of the alliance is the collective security guarantee against both external and internal threats. When ethnic conflicts in the Balkans posed a threat to the economic and political stability of Europe, it was NATO that brokered and enforced peace settlements after other organizations, including the European Union, the UN, and the Organization for Security and Cooperation in Europe, were unable to do so. When terrorists attacked the United States, NATO deployed airborne early-warning aircraft to help defend America and sent new troops to the Balkans to backfill for U.S. soldiers deployed to Afghanistan. Indeed, the military coordination and collaboration of a number of post–Cold War conflicts, including the first Gulf War, Kosovo, and Afghanistan, were possible because of the interoperability of NATO forces.

Just as NATO expanded to bring West Germany, a potential internal threat to Western Europe, into the framework of transatlantic security, successive NATO expansions have fulfilled the same mission, as former Cold War enemies have been brought into the alliance and special relationships have been developed with the successor states of the Soviet Union, including Russia and Ukraine. NATO's evolving role in Europe continues to be in line with Truman's vision of a broad and inclusive alliance.

Finally, NATO continues to keep the United States involved in European security. In spite of tensions over events such as the war with Iraq, the alliance remains an arena to reconcile European and American interests. While American politicians roundly criticized various European governments, Congress has also called on the Bush administration to utilize NATO assets in a variety of troubled regions, including the Middle East, South Asia, and Africa. As such, NATO continues to serve as an enduring legacy to Truman's internationalism and commitment to collective security.

Notes

[1] Lord Ismay was a driving force in the development of the United Nations and was the first secretary general.

[2] Harry S. Truman, *Memoirs,* vol. 2, *Years of Trial and Hope, 1946–1952* (1956; repr. New York: Signet, 1965), 134.

[3] Robert H. Ferrell, ed., *Off the Record: The Private Papers of Harry S. Truman* (New York: Harper & Row, 1980), 56–57.

[4] Arnold A. Offner, "Another Such Victory: President Truman, American Foreign Policy and the Cold War," *Diplomatic History* 23 (Spring 1999): 131–32.

[5] Chapter 8 of the UN charter allows for the creation of regional collective security bodies, Article 52, paragraph 2, calls for these regional bodies to serve as clearinghouses for conflicts before they are referred to the UN. United Nations, *Charter of the United Nations.* Department of State Bulletin, 24 June 1945, 1119–42; and Department of State Publication 2353, Conference Series 74.

[6] George F. Kennan [Mr. X, pseud.], "The Sources of Soviet Conduct," *Foreign Affairs* (July 1947): 566–82. Reprint, "The Sources of Soviet Conduct," *Foreign Affairs* 65 (Spring 1987): 852–68.

[7] George F. Kennan, *American Diplomacy, 1900–1950* (Chicago: University of Chicago Press, 1951), 111–12, 127–28.

[8] Dean Acheson, *Present at the Creation: My Years in the State Department* (New York: W. W. Norton, 1969), 725.

[9] Michael J. Hogan, *A Cross of Iron: Harry S. Truman and the Origins of the National Security State, 1945–1954* (Cambridge: Cambridge University Press, 1998), 465; and Melvyn P. Leffler, *A Preponderance of Power: National Security, the Truman Administration, and the Cold War* (Stanford: Stanford University Press, 1992), 99.

[10] Hogan, *Cross of Iron,* 464.

[11] Robert A. Taft, *A Foreign Policy for the Americas* (New York: Doubleday, 1951), esp. 11–20; Geoffrey Matthews, "Robert A. Taft, the Constitution and American Foreign Policy, 1939–1953," *Journal of Contemporary*

History 17 (July 1982): 515; Hogan, *Cross of Iron,* 464; and Vernon Van Dyke and Edward Lane Lewis, "Senator Taft and American Security," *Journal of Politics* (May 1952): 186.

[12] Paul Y. Hammond, *The Cold War Years: American Foreign Policy Since 1945* (New York: Harcourt, Brace & World, 1969), 35.

[13] Malcolm E. Jewell, "The Senate Republican Policy Committee and Foreign Policy," *Western Political Quarterly* 12 (December 1959): 969.

[14] Lester H. Brune contends that only with Truman's use of deficit spending could "the nation…afford both the Fair Deal and a larger military establishment without imposing hardship, denial and sacrifice on the American people. Guns *and* butter were both possible" (italics in the original). Brune, "Guns and Butter: The Pre–Korean War Dispute Over Budget Allocation," *American Journal of Economics and Sociology* 48 (July 1989): 367.

[15] John Gerard Ruggie argues that the multilateralist policies of the Cold War period were also a means to reconcile inward-focused domestic interests with international commitments. "The twentieth century drives by the United States to remake the world…were logical extensions of America's sense of the nature of its own community. For Wilson and Roosevelt alike, the vision of a multilateral world order provided the evocative vocabulary and justificatory ideas without which they found it difficult to imagine that the United States, a continental and largely self-sufficient power, would engage in any sustained international efforts beyond those commercial or humanitarian in nature." Ruggie, "Third Try at World Order? America and Multilateralism After the Cold War," *Political Science Quarterly* 109 (Fall 1994): 565.

[16] Lord Ismay, "Origins of the North Atlantic Treaty," in *NATO: The First Five Years, 1949–1954* (Paris: NATO, 1954) (also available through the NATO Archives at http://www.nato.int/archives, accessed 15 July 2003); and Robert Osgood, *NATO: The Entangling Alliance* (Chicago: University of Chicago Press, 1962), 29.

[17] Quoted in Osgood, *NATO,* 29.

[18] Truman, *Memoirs,* 2:280.

[19] Bernard Law Montgomery, *The Memoirs of Field Marshall Montgomery* (New York: World Publishing, 1958), 447.

[20] David Reynolds, "The European Dimension of the Cold War," in *Origins of the Cold War: An International History,* ed. Melvyn Leffler and David S. Painter (London: Routledge, 1994), 127.

[21] Lawrence S. Kaplan, *A Community of Interests: NATO and the Military Assistance Program, 1948–1951* (Washington DC: Office of the Secretary of Defense Historical Office, 1980), 17.

[22] Truman, *Memoirs,* 2:280–81; and National Security Council, "Position of US With Respect to Support for WU and Other Related Free Countries," (13 April 1948), cited in Kaplan, *Community of Interests,* 18.

[23] *The Vandenberg Resolution,* SR 239, 80th Congress, 2nd session, 11 June 1948 (available online at http://www.nato.int/docu/basics.htm, accessed 15 July 2003).

[24] Harry S. Truman, "Inaugural Address," (20 January 1949). Truman Presidential Library.

[25] Truman, *Memoirs,* 2:283–84; Cees Wiebes and Bert Zeeman, "The Origins of Western Defense: Belgian and Dutch Perspectives 1940–1949," in *The Atlantic Pact Forty Years Later: A Historical Reappraisal,* ed. Ehnio Di Nolfo (New York: Walter de Gruyter, 1991); and "Memorandum Recommending the Creation of a Collective Defense Agreement for the Nations of the North Atlantic From the Sixth Meeting of the United States–United Kingdom–Canada Security Conversations," 1 April 1948. Truman Papers: Staff Member and Office Files, Clark Clifford Files, Box 10, Truman Presidential Library.

[26] Geir Lundestad, *America, Scandinavia and the Cold War, 1945–1949* (New York: Columbia University Press, 1980); E. Timothy Smith, "United States Security and the Integration of Italy into the Western Bloc, 1947–1949," in *NATO: The Founding of the Atlantic Alliance and the Integration of Europe,* ed. John R. Gillingham and Francis Heller (New York: St. Martin's, 1992), 73–98; and Truman, *Memoirs,* 2:287.

[27] At a meeting on 11 March 1948, the Europeans requested $2 billion from the U.S., with the eventual possibility of up to $6 billion. See Kaplan, *Community of Interests,* 30.

[28] Antonio Varsori, "Great Britain and Italy, 1945–1956: The Partnership Between a Great Power and a Minor Power?" *Diplomacy and Statecraft* 3 (1992), 206; Martin H. Folly, "Britain and the Issue of Italian Membership in NATO, 1948–49," *Review of International Studies* 13 (1987): 177–96; and Armand Bernard, quoted in Bruna Bagnato, "France and the Origins of the Atlantic Pact," in Di Nolfo, *The Atlantic Pact Forty Years Later,* 103.

[29] Dean Acheson, "Speech on the Proposed North Atlantic Treaty" (reading copy), 18 March 1949, Dean Acheson Papers, Box 84, Truman Presidential Library. Truman had already seen and added comments and revisions to the initial draft of the Washington Treaty, which was completed on 24 December 1948; see "Proposed North Atlantic Security Arrangement," 14 January 1949, Truman Papers: President's Secretary's Files, Box 132, Truman Presidential Library.

[30] NATO, *The North Atlantic Treaty,* Article 5, Washington DC, 4 April 1949, U.S. Statutes at Large, 63, Part 2, 2241. (available online at http//www.nato.int/docu.basics.htm, accessed 15 July 2003).

[31] Harry S. Truman, "Speech at the Signing Ceremony" (draft copy), 1 April 1949, Truman Papers: President's Secretary's Files, Box 48, Truman Presidential Library.

[32] Tony Smith, *America's Mission: The United States and the Worldwide Struggle for Democracy in the Twentieth Century* (Princeton: Princeton University Press, 1994), 6, 10.

[33] White House, Press Release (12 April 1949), Staff Member and Office Files, Box 7, Truman Presidential Library.

[34] John Spanier and Steven W. Hook, *American Foreign Policy Since World War II,* 14th (Washington DC: Congressional Quarterly Press, 1998), 63.

[35] Truman, *Memoirs,* 2:289.

[36] Ibid.

[37] House Foreign Relations Committee, *The Mutual Defense Assistance Act of 1949. Hearings on HR 5748 and HR 5895,* 81st Congr., 1st sess., 3 January 1949, 71, 82.

[38] Edward Furdson, *The European Defense Community: A History* (London: Macmillan, 1980), 114–15; and Harry S. Truman, "Statement on June 27, 1950," *Department of State Bulletin* 22 (3 July 1950): 5.

[39] The European allies, led by Denmark, the Netherlands, and Norway, were particularly opposed to Turkish membership in NATO; see Mark Smith, *NATO Enlargement During the Cold War: Strategy and System in the Western Alliance* (New York: Palgrave, 2000), esp. 62–95. Omar Bradley, however, argued strongly in favor of Greek and Turkish membership; see Omar N. Bradley, "Memorandum for the President" (18 October 1951), 1–3, President's Secretary's Files, Box 48, Truman Presidential Library.

[40] NATO, North Atlantic Council, "Final Communique," New York Conference (18 September 1950) Department of State, Bulletin, 2 October 1950, 530–31; Kaplan, *Community of Interests,* 148; Gaddis Smith, *American Secretaries of State and Their Diplomacy: Dean Acheson* (New York: Cooper Square, 1972), 16:252; and Harry S. Truman, "Statement by the President," Press Release (5 April 1951), Truman Papers President's Secretary's Files, Box 48, Truman Presidential Library.

[41] NATO, North Atlantic Council, "Final Communique," Washington Conference (18 November 1949); and NATO, North Atlantic Council, "Final Communique," London Conference, (18 May 1950), Department of State Bulletin, 29 May 1950, 830–31.

[42] NSC-68 set the date as 1954, but the Joint Chiefs of Staff continued to use 1952 as the point of maximum threat; see U.S. Senate, Committee on Appropriations, *Hearings, Department of Defense Appropriations for 1953* (Washington DC: Government Printing Office, 1953), 332–35, 385; and U.S. Congress, "For a Strong and Free World," *Quarterly Reports to Congress on the Mutual Security Act* 1 (Washington DC: Government Printing Office, 1951), 5.

[43] Harry S. Truman, "Statement by the President," Press Release (9 September 1950); U.S. Department of State, "Communique of the US, U.K. and French Foreign Ministers," (19 September 1950), *Department of State Bulletin* 23 (2 October 1950), 530–31; and NATO, Supreme Allied Commander Europe, *First Annual Report* (Brussels: NATO, 1951), 2.

[44] Dean Acheson, "Telegram to the President," 14 September 1950, President's Secretary's Files, Truman Presidential Library.

[45] See Konrad Adenauer, *Memoirs, 1945–1966* (Chicago: Henry Regnery, 1966); U.S. Office of the High Commissioner for Germany, Office of the Executive Secretary, *History of the Allied High Commission for Germany* (Washington DC: Government Printing Office, 1951); and Federal Republic of Germany, *Government Declaration by the German Federal*

Chancellor, Dr. Konrad Adenauer, Before the German Bundestag on 20 October 1953 (Bonn: Press & Information Office, 1953).

[46]"Pactomania" refers to initiatives of Secretary of State John Foster Dulles and his efforts to initiate security treaties with a variety of states in the 1950s. Ruggie, "Third Try," 558–59.

LEADING THROUGH MULTILATERALISM

The United Nations and the National Security Legacy of President Truman

Meena Bose

> It will be just as easy for nations to get along in a republic of the world as it is for us to get along in the republic of the United States.
>
> —Harry S. Truman, 28 June 1945

President Harry S. Truman took office unexpectedly on 12 April 1945, just three months before he made the above statement about the United Nations, and his preparation for the position of chief executive was limited. Although he had served in the Senate for ten years, and was of course vice president at the time of Franklin D. Roosevelt's death, Truman was not a member of FDR's inner circle. Thus, he had not participated in debates about World War II, the creation of the United Nations, or the atomic bomb. As senator, Truman had served on the Military Affairs Committee and the Military Subcommittee of the Appropriations Committee. In 1941, he spearheaded the creation of the Special Committee to Investigate the National Defense Program, popularly known as the Truman Committee, which oversaw the awarding of defense contracts, seeking to reduce inefficiency and waste. Nevertheless, Truman did not become president with a defined foreign policy agenda.

By the time Truman left office in 1953, the world had changed dramatically. The Allied Powers successfully defeated the Axis Powers in World War II, and in the heady aftermath of victory, the prospects for working together to prevent another war seemed great. Thus, in 1945, the United States and fifty other nations created the United Nations to promote international peace and stability. But the wartime alliance of the United States and the Soviet Union would not last, and Cold War politics soon overshadowed the international institution. With the Truman Doctrine and the Marshall Plan, the Truman administration committed the United States to assisting its allies in fighting the encroachment of Communism, and to rebuilding Western Europe. The creation of the North Atlantic Treaty Organization (NATO) in 1949 ensured that the United States was bound to defend member states in the event of aggression from the Soviet Union or other nations. Most importantly, the Truman administration's Cold War strategy of containment, which sought to keep Communism within existing borders, set the stage for U.S. foreign policy in the next forty years.

Scholars of the Truman presidency most often focus on containment, the Truman Doctrine, the Marshall Plan, and NATO in identifying Truman's national security legacy. An area that has received less systematic attention is Truman's use of the UN. After presiding over the creation of the UN, Truman initially kept the institution at arm's length, operating largely through the secretary of state in his dealings with UN matters. But when North Korea invaded South Korea in June 1950, Truman and his advisors immediately went to the UN to seek resolutions condemning the attack and then authorizing the use of force to repel North Korean forces from South Korea. Truman, in fact, operated solely through the UN and did not seek congressional authorization to support the use of force in Korea. Thus, Truman's national security legacy also includes the first example of sustained collective action by the United Nations in employing force to restore international peace and stability.

This chapter examines why Truman chose to operate through the United Nations in the Korean War, and the consequences of his actions for U.S. national security policy making today. Given the Bush administration's decision in February and March 2003 not to seek a resolution from the UN authorizing the use of force in Iraq, an analysis of the Truman administration's decision to seek UN support for the Korean War is both timely and necessary. In particular, this chapter focuses on two questions: First, why did Truman seek a UN resolution authorizing the use of force in Korea? Second, why did Truman decide not to seek a congressional resolution supporting the war?

TRUMAN AND THE CREATION OF THE UN

Although Truman was not involved in the debates leading up to the creation of the UN, as president he brought the United States into the UN, and he supported the organization from the outset. When the Cold War began shortly after World War II, prospects for the UN to serve as an effective international organization seemed dim. Yet the United States served as one of the founding leaders of the organization, and without U.S. determination to see the UN succeed, as demonstrated foremost by FDR and then Truman, the organization likely would not have come into being.

The U.S. interest in joining an international organization dated back to the failure of the Wilson administration to gain Senate ratification for the Treaty of Versailles after World War I. The treaty endorsed the creation of a League of Nations, which would seek to prevent future world wars by resolving international disputes first through political and economic means, using force as a last resort. Senators objected to the possibility that the treaty might permit a president to send troops to support a

President Truman addressing the closing session of the United Nations Conference on International Organization, June 1945. (TPL, 64-579-5)

League action without getting congressional support. Senator Henry Cabot Lodge, in particular, opposed ratifying the treaty without including fourteen reservations that would ensure U.S. sovereignty in decision making. Although the treaty won a majority of votes in the Senate, it did not gain the two-thirds necessary for ratification, despite going before the Senate twice, in 1919 and again in 1920.[1]

During World War II, the United States began to reconsider the possibility of helping to create an international organization. (The League of Nations, which was created without U.S. participation, did not become an effective instrument for international coordination and grew steadily weaker through the 1930s.) In 1943, members of both the House and the Senate passed resolutions calling for "the creation of appropriate international machinery with power adequate to establish and to maintain a just and lasting peace, among the nations of the world."[2] In October 1943, the United States, United Kingdom, Soviet Union, and China approved the Moscow Declaration, which called for creating an international organization to ensure "international peace and stability." The following year, leaders of these nations met in Washington DC (in what became known as the Dumbarton Oaks Conference) to pursue the idea further, concluding that the guiding premise of the organization should be "the principle of the sovereign equality of all peace-loving states."[3]

In the spring of 1945, the United States hosted a nine-week conference in San Francisco that focused on the task of drafting a charter for the new organization. Fifty nations participated, including the Soviet Union. The United States insisted on Soviet support for the incipient organization, and Soviet Foreign Minister Vyacheslav Molotov even visited Washington DC on his way to the conference. The U.S. delegation included eight members, of which two came from the House and two from the Senate. Truman, newly sworn in as president of the United States, spoke to the opening session of the conference by radio and stoutly declared the necessity of an international institution to promote peace and security. As he noted, "Man has learned long ago that it is impossible to live unto himself. This same basic principle applies today to nations. We were not isolated during the war. We dare not now become isolated in peace."[4]

Delegates to the San Francisco conference worked from April through June 1945 to draft the UN charter, which was signed by representatives of the fifty participating nations on 26 June 1945. (Poland did not participate in the conference, but it did sign the treaty soon after and is considered one of the original member states.)[5] Speaking in Kansas City, Missouri, two months after the charter was signed, Truman expressed confidence in the potential of the new organization to facilitate cooperation among states. Here he made the well-known statement quoted at the beginning of this chapter. The president was paraphrasing Alfred Lord Tennyson's poem "Locksley Hall," which he knew well—he had kept ten lines of the poem in his wallet since 1910.

On 2 July 1945, Truman presented the charter of the United Nations to the Senate and endorsed its ratification, stating, "This Charter points down the only road to enduring peace. There is no other."[6] The subsequent Senate Foreign Relations Committee hearings to review the charter focused particularly on what role Congress would play in decisions to use U.S. troops to enforce UN policies. Although Truman was in Potsdam negotiating post–World War II matters with British prime minister Winston Churchill (replaced during the conference by newly elected prime minister Clement Attlee) and Soviet leader Josef Stalin, he took the time to communicate with the Senate about sending troops abroad. He promised that "when any such agreement or agreements are negotiated, it will be my purpose to ask the Congress for appropriate legislation to approve them."[7]

The Senate ultimately approved the UN charter with only two dissenting votes in 1945. A majority of the other member states did the same in the next few months, and on 24 October 1945, the UN officially was established. Congress soon invited the UN to locate within the United States; John D. Rockefeller Jr. purchased land in New York City and deeded it to the UN. Four years later, the UN General Assembly met in an open-air session in New York City, and Truman spoke at the event. The Truman administration's commitment to maintaining U.S. support for the UN was clear.

TRUMAN AND THE UN—THE EARLY YEARS

The early years of the UN present a mixed record on international cooperation and the role of the UN in the making of U.S. foreign policy. Perhaps the most significant achievement of the UN was the creation of Israel in 1948. The UN also oversaw the withdrawal of Soviet troops from Iran in 1946 and the partition of Korea in 1947/48. But Cold War politics hindered UN action in many other areas, such as international control of atomic energy. From the U.S. perspective, the UN was a useful agency for debate, but it did not provide a forum for U.S. policy making. Indeed, the U.S. representative to the UN Security Council, former senator Warren R. Austin, reported to the secretary of state and did not participate in key national security debates. Austin represented the United States in UN discussions, but he played a limited role in U.S. foreign policy. In many respects, Austin's role in the Truman administration paralleled the UN's role in U.S. foreign policy making.

The structure of the UN explains some of the impediments to multilateral coordination. The UN was supposed to mark the "development of a dynamic international society" and provide "an atmosphere and means for adjustment," but the actual UN institutions do not always facilitate such interaction. The legislative branch of the UN contains both the General Assembly and the

Truman looks on as Secretary of State Edward Stettinius signs the UN charter in San Francisco, 26 June 1945. (TPL, 64-579-7)

Security Council. Senator Arthur H. Vandenberg once described the General Assembly as the "town meeting of the world," because all member states have an equal voice and vote in debates.[8]

The Security Council addresses questions of peace and security, and is composed of fifteen members—five permanent and ten rotating, who are chosen by the General Assembly for two-year terms. Each of the permanent members—the United States, Great Britain, France, China, and Russia (Soviet Union from 1945 to 1991)—reserves veto power on any Security Council action. Former secretary of state and first U.S. ambassador to the UN Edward R. Stettinius Jr. declared that the veto "simply recognizes the power facts of life," but in so doing, it also mounts a significant obstacle to international action. In the first decade of the UN's existence, for example, the Soviet Union employed its veto in the Security Council more than sixty times.[9]

Truman had appointed Stettinius as the first U.S. ambassador to the UN in 1945 because of his leading role in creating the organization. Stettinius initially hoped that he would serve as a key conduit between the president and the UN, but Truman worked directly with new secretary of state James Byrnes, not with Stettinius. In June 1946, Stettinius resigned, telling Truman that with "the State Department determining policy on Security Council affairs, I am just not needed."[10] A foreign service officer replaced Stettinius for the rest of the year and in 1947 Austin, who had retired from the Senate, became the U.S. ambassador.

Truman hoped that his bipartisan appointment would assuage concerns of the Republican-controlled Congress about U.S. policies at the UN. A strong anti–New Deal Republican, Austin had joined the Senate in 1931, and though he differed with FDR on domestic policy, he strongly supported the president's actions in World War II. He joined the Senate Foreign Relations Committee in 1944 (a position he had long sought but which earlier isolationist Republican leaders had refused to give him), and there he concentrated on the role of the United States in the postwar world. A supporter of the UN Charter, Trade Agreements Act, and Bretton Woods Agreement, Austin clearly was committed to an internationalist U.S. foreign policy.

Once in office, however, Austin faced some of the same difficulties as Stettinius in shaping the president's agenda. As State Department officials paid less attention to the UN, Austin's policy-making role became further circumscribed. His biographer writes that Austin's "personal faith in the role of the United Nations, while respected by other Department members, was out of line with their attitudes toward the development of actual policy." Austin did not participate in the development of the Truman Doctrine, which provided aid to Greece and Turkey, nor was he aware of the "Long Telegram" that George Kennan sent to Truman from Moscow in February 1946 about the Soviet Union's postwar intentions. Consequently, Austin was not involved in the primary focus of U.S. foreign policy, namely, the development of Truman's containment strategy toward the Soviet Union. Instead, Austin served as "spokesman for American policy with little influence on the policy making process."[11]

One example of Austin's distance from U.S. foreign policy making is the Truman administration's role in the creation of Israel. In early 1947, Great Britain announced that the UN would address the question of who would control Palestine. On 29 November 1947, the UN General Assembly voted to partition Palestine between Arabs and Jews, and to keep Jerusalem separate. Because Arab nations strongly opposed the plan, the State Department suggested that the UN should serve as a trustee for Palestine and postpone partition. In March 1948, Austin recommended in the Security Council that the UN "propos[e] suspension of partition and a temporary trusteeship." Truman was furious, writing in his diary, "This morning I find that the State Dept. has reversed my Palestine policy." The president immediately declared that trusteeship was not an acceptable substitute for partition, and in May 1948, the White House told the State Department that Truman would recognize Israel as soon as the state was proclaimed. Austin learned of this decision from the State Department's Director of the Office of United Nations Affairs, Dean Rusk, not from the White House. The entire U.S. delegation at the UN was so angry that Rusk had to go to New York personally to keep them from resigning.[12]

While the Truman administration's response to UN actions on Israel was mixed, the administration itself sought UN assistance in establishing a government in Korea. After the defeat of Japan in World War II, the United States and Soviet Union shared the occupation of Korea, dividing their responsibilities at the thirty-eighth parallel, in the middle of the country. In 1947, the United States persuaded the UN General Assembly to pass a resolution calling for each country to hold elections in its zone to create a national assembly, supervised by the UN Temporary Commission on Korea. But the Soviet Union rejected this proposal, so elections took place only in the South, which elected Syngman Rhee as president of the Republic of Korea, or South Korea. In December 1948, the General Assembly declared that the republic was "the only such [lawful] government in Korea." The Soviet Union separately established the Korean Democratic People's Republic, or North Korea, in 1948, led by Kim Il-sung. U.S. Ambassador Austin was not active in these debates due to surgery and convalescence from November 1948 through January 1949.[13]

On the whole, Austin did not influence foreign policy making in the Truman administration significantly. He was not a member of the National Security Council, nor did he participate in innercircle deliberations of Truman's national security team. Ill health also hindered Austin's involvement in UN debates. In 1951, Austin developed a serious respiratory problem that required long-term recuperation; during Truman's final year in office, Austin's deputy, Ernest Gross, primarily represented the United States at the UN. Philip C. Jessup, a member of the U.S. delegation to the UN General Assembly, wrote to Secretary of State Dean Acheson in December 1951 that when Austin first became ill, "there was a good deal of evidence of mental strain in terms of a feeling that he had been ignored and put to one side and had not been a real participant in making important policy decisions."[14] Although Jessup continued that Austin no longer expressed such sentiments, the initial statement aptly illustrates Austin's role in the policy-making process. Still, routine correspondence indicates that Austin, Acheson, and Truman maintained cordial and friendly relations throughout the administration.[15]

The early years of the UN thus witnessed participation by the United States on key issues such as the creation of Israel and the partition of Korea. For the most part, however, Truman and his advisors made major policy decisions through their usual channels, rather than operating through the UN. With the advent of the Cold War, the UN seemed increasingly likely to fall into the shadows of U.S.–Soviet conflict, serving more as a forum for discussion than an effective policy-making authority. The Korean War, however, firmly entrenched the UN's role in international conflict resolution.

THE KOREAN WAR—TRUMAN'S DECISION
TO WORK THROUGH THE UN

When North Korea invaded South Korea on 25 June 1950, the U.S. reaction was immediate and unequivocal. Within three days, the United States had sponsored two resolutions in the UN Security Council criticizing the invasion and authorizing the use of force to restore the balance of power on the peninsula. The president was steadfast in his decision to operate through the UN, and his national security team supported, indeed encouraged, this approach. In so doing, the Truman administration established the precedent that the UN would serve as the venue for authorizing military force in the international arena to respond to the invasion of one state by another.

The reasons for North Korea's invasion are complex and beyond the scope of this analysis, but they included both Cold War politics as well as internal disputes on the Korean peninsula. From the U.S. perspective, the need to uphold the integrity of South Korea, as established by UN resolution after World War II, was clear. Secretary of State Dean Acheson received a telephone call at home in the evening of 24 June 1950 (U.S. time), informing him of the invasion. He quickly telephoned the president, who was vacationing in Independence, Missouri. Truman approved Acheson's recommendation that the United States request an emergency session of the UN Security Council the next day to call for a cease-fire. The president made immediate plans to return to Washington.[16]

By the time Truman left for Washington on 25 June, the Security Council had met and unanimously approved a U.S.–sponsored resolution "condemning the North Korean attack and calling for the withdrawal of their forces from below the thirty-eighth parallel."[17] Of the eleven members of the Security Council, nine approved the resolution; Yugoslavia abstained and the Soviet Union was absent. The latter had boycotted the United Nations for the previous six months to protest the organization's decision not to extend membership to communist China. Had the Soviet Union participated in the debate on Korea, it certainly could have exercised its veto power to reject the resolution. But it did not and to this day, "no one is exactly certain why [Soviet leader Josef] Stalin did not try to thwart the U.S. in the Security

Council."[18] Nevertheless, the Soviet absence from Security Council deliberations ensured a unified response to the invasion.

Truman's trip back to Washington took three hours, which gave the president plenty of time to reflect upon the invasion and the necessary U.S. response. His reading of history made clear that the United States could not permit this aggression to continue unchecked. As Truman recorded in his memoirs:

> In my generation, this was not the first occasion when the strong attacked the weak. I recalled some earlier instances: Manchuria, Ethiopia, Austria. I remembered how each time that the democracies failed to act, it had encouraged the aggressors to keep going ahead. Communism was acting in Korea just as Hitler, Mussolini, and the Japanese had acted ten, fifteen, and twenty years earlier. I felt certain that if South Korea was allowed to fall, Communist leaders would be emboldened to override nations closer to our own shores.[19]

Truman also demonstrated his personal commitment to the UN, both in his memoirs and in his discussions with his national security team upon returning to Washington. He wrote in his memoirs, "The foundations and principles of the United Nations were at stake unless this unprovoked attack on Korea could be stopped."[20] On the evening of 25 June 1950, Truman met with State and Defense Department officials as well as the Joint Chiefs of Staff and military service secretaries at Blair House. Truman insisted that the group have dinner before discussing the invasion, and in casual conversation before the meal, the president affirmed his support of the UN. One participant recalls hearing Truman say, "We can't let the UN down!"[21]

At Truman's request, Acheson led the Blair House discussion, focusing on what military assistance the United States might provide to South Korea and proposing consideration of a second Security Council resolution to authorize such support. The Joint Chiefs of Staff discussed the possibility of Soviet intervention in the war as well as the need to protect Formosa (now Taiwan). Truman stressed that the U.S. was "working entirely for the United Nations" and "would wait for further action until the UN order [was] flouted."[22] As the meeting came to a close, Truman reiterated the point: "It [the United Nations] was our idea, and in this first big test, we just can't let them down." He later noted in his memoirs, "There was no suggestion from anyone that either the

United Nations or the United States could back away from [the invasion]. This was the test of all the talk of the last five years of collective security."[23]

The next day Truman released a statement summarizing U.S. actions in response to the North Korean invasion. He expressed support for the Security Council's order that North Korean forces withdraw from South Korea, and he added that "in accordance with the resolution of the Security Council, the United States will vigorously support the effort of the Council to terminate this serious breach of the peace." Reaffirming his commitment to upholding UN decisions, Truman concluded that "willful disregard of the obligation to keep the peace cannot be tolerated by nations that support the United Nations Charter."[24]

Truman and his advisory team recognized that the UN resolution calling for the withdrawal of North Korean troops from South Korea would have to be backed up with force. Truman met again on 26 June with top officials from the State Department, Defense Department, and Joint Chiefs of Staff, who recommended a second resolution from the Security Council that would authorize assistance to repel the North Korean attack. The prospect of a Soviet veto of the resolution would not deter U.S. action, as the United States would then state that it was acting "in support of the [UN] Charter." Truman later recalled that "the Republic of Korea needed help at once if it was not to be overrun." Acheson also recommended that Truman meet with congressional leaders to inform them of decisions regarding Korea, and Truman said he would be seeing them the following morning.[25]

On 27 June, the UN Security Council passed a second resolution authorizing the use of force to restore peace in Korea. Ambassador Austin, who had been vacationing in Vermont when the war began, was not present for the 25 June Security Council meeting, but he returned to New York in time to introduce the 27 June resolution. He declared that the war marked "the gravest crisis in [the UN's] existence," and that U.S. actions represented "support of the United Nation's purposes and principles—in a word: 'peace.'" The second Security Council resolution passed 7 to 1, with Yugoslavia opposed, the Soviet Union absent, and Egypt and India abstaining. (Egypt eventually opposed the resolution, while India supported it.) Soon after, Truman authorized the use of U.S. combat forces in Korea.[26] A few weeks later, he formally thanked Acheson for operating through the UN, writing:

Your initiative in immediately calling the Security Council of the U.N. on Saturday night and notifying me was the key to what followed afterwards. Had you not acted promptly in that direction we would have had to go into Korea alone. ...Your handling of the situation since has been superb. I'm sending you this for your record.[27]

Truman's actions and his note to Acheson illustrate his steadfast support for working through the UN to restore the boundaries of South Korea. Acheson's skillful diplomacy enabled the United States to lead two resolutions through the Security Council, one condemning the North Korean invasion and a second authorizing the use of military force to repel the attack. The resolutions marked a turning point in the history of the United States and the UN. As David McCullough writes, "For the first time in history, a world organization had voted to use armed force to stop armed force."[28] Notably absent from Truman's deliberations, however, was his counterpart in government, namely, the Congress. This aspect of Truman's decision-making process would spark far more criticism over the long term.

THE KOREAN WAR—CONGRESS'S ROLE IN DECISION MAKING

In 1950, Truman's decision to seek UN, not congressional, support for sending U.S. troops to combat the North Korean invasion was widely accepted by the public as well as members of Congress. Truman did meet with congressional leaders in the week following the invasion to inform them of his administration's plans, but he decided that explicit congressional authorization of his actions was unnecessary. Some members of Congress were critical of this choice at the time, but for the most part, immediate critiques of the president's actions were muted. As the war continued, however, and prospects for a quick resolution became grim, congressional critics grew more vocal about the president's decision to keep them out of the policy-making loop.

On 27 June 1950, Truman invited congressional leaders to the White House for a briefing on Korea by State and Defense Department officials. Members of the House and Senate Foreign Relations and Armed Services Committees attended the meeting. Truman told the group that the meeting would serve to "describe the situation in the Far East to them, and inform them of a number of important decisions he had made during the previous twenty-four hours, and to read to them a statement which he intended to release in a matter of minutes to the press." After Acheson summarized U.S. actions in response to the North Korean invasion, Truman stated that "the communist invasion of South Korea could not be let pass by unnoticed. ... We had to make a stand some time, or else let all of Asia go by the board."[29]

In response to congressional queries, Truman and Acheson confirmed that the United States was acting in support of UN decisions. Tom Connally, chairman of the Senate Committee on Foreign Relations, remarked that "this was the clearest test case that the United Nations has ever faced...and if the United Nations cannot bring the crisis in Korea to an end, then we might just as well wash up the United Nations and forget it."[30] Truman again assured the group that the United States would act under UN auspices.

Immediately after the meeting, Truman released a statement criticizing North Korea for having "defied the orders of the Security Council of the United Nations issued to preserve international peace and security," and calling for U.S. forces in the Far East to provide military assistance to Formosa, the Philippines, and Indochina.[31] Widespread praise followed the president's announcement, and Congress immediately passed a bill to extend selective service by one year with votes of 315 to 4 in the House and 76 to 0 in the Senate.[32] The public deluged the White House and Congress with letters, telegrams, and phone calls expressing support, and newspaper editorials lauded the president for his courageous leadership. As the *Washington Post* wrote, "These are days calling for steady nerves, for a strict eye on the ball, and for a renewed resolve to keep our purposes pure. ...The occasion has found the man in Harry Truman."[33] Truman met again with congressional leaders on 30 June to explain his decision to send ground forces to Korea, and Democrats and Republicans alike expressed their support for the president.

At the same time, Truman did face some criticism in the summer of 1950 for informing, rather than consulting and getting authorization from Congress on the use of U.S. troops in Korea. As early as 28 June, Robert Taft spoke on the Senate floor to criticize Truman's failure to request a resolution from Congress. As Taft said, Truman "has brought war about without consulting Congress and without congressional approval. ...[This] seems to me...a complete usurpation by the President of authority to use the Armed Forces of this country." Taft said that he would support a declaration of war and that the Constitution required such authorization from Congress. At Truman's 30 June meeting with congressional leaders, Senate Minority Leader Kenneth Wherry asked why Truman had not consulted with Congress before deciding to send ground troops to Korea. Truman simply replied, "I just had to act as Commander-in-Chief, and I did."[34]

As the war continued, criticism of Truman's decision not to seek a congressional resolution increased. In December 1951, Senator Arthur V. Watkins (R-UT) published an article in the *Western Political Quarterly* titled "War by Executive Order." Watkins wrote that when Truman decided to take military action in Korea,

> there was no consultation with Congress nor was Congressional approval sought. The decisions were made on behalf of the United States by the Executive Department of the Government. ...The President circumvented both the Constitution of the United States and the Charter of the United Nations and bypassed the Congress when he committed the armed forces of the United States to war in Korea.[35]

A 1951 Senate debate concluded that Truman's action failed to comply with either the UN Charter or administration promises to Congress, and that the war "was an American, not a UN, operation."[36] Because of the protracted war, Truman decided not to run for reelection in 1952. The elections that year resulted in the Democratic party losing the presidency for the first time since FDR took office in 1933; the Democrats also lost both chambers of Congress. Truman's public approval rating reached a high of 87 percent in June 1945; when he left office, it had fallen to 31 percent.[37]

Truman likely decided not to seek a congressional resolution authorizing the use of force in Korea for several reasons. Partisanship may have been one concern; as Truman biographer Alonzo Hamby writes, "The Republicans would give him their backing only after ventilating every mistake and failure in American Far Eastern policy, thoroughly trashing his Department of State, and attempting to force Acheson's resignation." Respected historians, including Henry Steele Commager and Arthur M. Schlesinger Jr., have defended Truman's actions and said the president did not require congressional approval to send troops abroad. Truman himself told reporters at a 29 June 1950 press conference that "we are not at war," and instead endorsed a reporter's phrase that sending troops to Korea marked "a police action under the United Nations." Perhaps most importantly, Truman himself thought the powers of the executive office justified his policies. As Truman aide George M. Elsey later said, "It is quite certain that the President would never have asked for a resolution."[38]

Truman's decision to seek UN authorization for the use of force to repel the North Korean invasion in 1950 clearly established the organization as a force in international affairs. Truman and his national security team did not view the UN as a participant in U.S. foreign policy making, but they did consider the UN to be a useful venue for building an international coalition to support U.S. actions. Truman's representatives at the UN did not assume policy-making roles, but they conveyed the administration's proposals effectively to their counterparts from other nations. Certainly the political environment of the time contributed to Truman's success in working through the UN—had the Soviet Union been seated at the Security Council in June 1950, it almost certainly would have vetoed the two resolutions on Korea. Nevertheless, Truman's willingness to make use of the opportunity to garner international backing for his foreign policy agenda makes the legitimacy of the UN in endorsing international action part of his national security legacy.

At the same time, Truman's decision not to seek congressional authorization for sending U.S. troops to Korea continues to be questioned today. As one scholar writes, "A resolution of congressional support would not have precluded eventual criticism of the war, but it would have put some constraints on that opposition." Today, Truman's failure to get official congressional support on Korea ranks along with the lack of a congressional declaration of war in Vietnam as a textbook example of what Arthur M. Schlesinger Jr. later called "the imperial presidency."[39] While a congressional resolution in 1950 would have required the Truman administration to spend some political capital, it likely would have passed without difficulty. Truman's failure to get congressional backing reflected the predominant view of presidential power in foreign policy at the time, but it has not withstood the scrutiny of history.

Recent events in American politics demonstrate that presidents well understand both aspects of Truman's legacy on military intervention. In 1990–91, President George H. W. Bush won both UN and congressional support—although he maintained throughout that he did not require the latter—for the use of force to repel Iraq's invasion of Kuwait. In 2002–3, President George W. Bush secured a congressional resolution authorizing the use of force to pursue "regime change" in Iraq and depose Saddam Hussein, but he was not able to win explicit UN backing for military force (though the Security Council did pass unanimously one resolution promising "serious consequences" if Hussein did not comply with earlier UN resolutions on disarmament). The validity of the second Bush's decision to go ahead with war despite the lack of UN endorsement continues to be debated.

In the future, presidents may benefit from reviewing how Truman and his advisors successfully shepherded through the Security Council the two resolutions calling for the restoration of peace in Korea and authorizing military force to achieve that goal. That accomplishment forms a cornerstone of Truman's national security legacy. As Truman himself said in 1950, "The United Nations action in Korea is of supreme importance for all the peoples of the world. ... This is a tremendous step forward in the age-old struggle to establish the rule of law in the world."[40]

NOTES

The views expressed herein are those of the author and do not purport to reflect the position of the United States Military Academy, the Department of the Army, or the Department of Defense.

[1] Louis Fisher, "The Korean War: On What Legal Basis Did Truman Act?" *American Journal of International Law* 89 (January 1995): 22–23.

[2] The quotation is taken from the House resolution; the Senate passed a similar resolution a few weeks later. See Fisher, "The Korean War," 24–25.

[3] Fisher, "The Korean War," 25; and Benjamin H. Brown and Joseph E. Johnson, *The U.S. and the U.N.* (New York: Foreign Policy Association, 1954), 10–11.

[4] Robert J. Donovan, *Conflict and Crisis: The Presidency of Harry S. Truman, 1945–1948* (New York: W. W. Norton, 1977), 49. See also,

"Address to the United Nations Conference in San Francisco," 25 April 1945, in *Public Papers of the Presidents, 1945* (Washington DC: Government Printing Office, 1961), 20–23.

[5] *Basic Facts About the United Nations* (New York: United Nations, Department of Public Information, 1995), 3.

[6] Address of Harry S. Truman to U.S. Senate, 2 July 1945, and UN Charter, 2 July 1945, Official File, White House Central Files. Reprinted in Dennis Merrill, ed., *Documentary History of the Truman Presidency,* vol. 35, *The United Nations, 1945–1953: The Development of a World Organization* (Bethesda, MD: University Publications of America, 2002), 153–97.

[7] Fisher, "The Korean War," 27–28.

[8] Clark M. Eichelberger, *U.N.: The First Ten Years* (New York: Harper & Brothers, 1955), 8–9; and Brown and Johnson, *The U.S. and the U.N.*, 11.

[9] Eichelberger, *The U.N.,* 14. See also *Basic Facts About the United Nations,* 3–19.

[10] Thomas M. Campbell and George C. Herring, eds. *The Diaries of Edward R. Stettinius Jr., 1943–1946* (New York: New Viewpoints, 1975), 473.

[11] George T. Mazuzan, *Warren R. Austin at the U.N., 1946–1953* (Kent, OH: Kent State University Press, 1977), 185; on Austin's outsider role during the development of Truman's containment policy, see 72, 87.

[12] Alonzo L. Hamby, *Man of the People: A Life of Harry S. Truman* (New York: Oxford University Press, 1995), 412, 416–17.

[13] Gary R. Hess, *Presidential Decisions for War: Korea, Vietnam, and the Persian Gulf* (Baltimore: Johns Hopkins University Press, 2001), 11; and Mazuzan, *Austin at the U.N.,* 116–17.

[14] Mazuzan, *Austin at the U.N.,* 178; and Philip C. Jessup to Dean Acheson, 11 December 1951, Dean Acheson Papers, Truman Presidential Library.

[15] See "Correspondence or Summaries of Conversations with Austin, Warren T.," Memorandums of Conversation Index, 1949–53, Acheson Papers, Truman Presidential Library; and "Austin, Warren T. File," President's Personal File, 1945–53, White House Central File, Truman Presidential Library.

[16] Dean Acheson, *Present at the Creation: My Years in the State Department* (New York: W. W. Norton, 1969), 402–4.

[17] Hess, *Presidential Decisions for War,* 8–9.

[18] Arnold A. Offner, *Another Such Victory: President Truman and the Cold War, 1945–1953* (Stanford: Stanford University Press, 2002), 372.

[19] Harry S. Truman, *Memoirs,* vol. 2, *Years of Trial and Hope* (Garden City, NY: Doubleday, 1956), 332–33.

[20] Ibid., 2:333.

[21] Quoted in Philip C. Jessup, *The Birth of Nations* (New York: Columbia University Press, 1974), 10.

[22] Memorandum of Conversation, "Korean Situation," 25 June 1950, Acheson Papers, Truman Presidential Library.

[23] McCullough, *Truman,* 779; and Truman, *Memoirs,* 2:334. For a summary by one of the meeting participants, see James E. Webb to John W. Snyder, 25 April 1975, James E. Webb Papers, Truman Presidential Library.

[24] Statement by the President, 26 June 1950, George M. Elsey Papers, Truman Presidential Library. Also available in *Public Papers of the Presidents: Harry S. Truman, 1950* (Washington DC: Government Printing Office, 1965), 491–92.

[25] Memorandum of Conversation, "Korean Situation," 26 June 1950, Acheson Papers, Truman Presidential Library; Truman, *Memoirs,* 2:337; and Acheson, *Present at the Creation,* 408.

[26] Mazuzan, *Austin at the U.N.,* 147, 149; and Hess, *Presidential Decisions for War,* 25–30. See also Security Council Official Records, 474th meeting, 27 June, 1950, "Selected Records Relating to the Korean War," Truman Papers, Truman Presidential Library.

[27] McCullough, *Truman,* 783. See also, Dean Acheson, *The Korean War* (New York: W. W. Norton, 1971), 34.

[28] McCullough, *Truman,* 781.

[29] Memorandum, Meeting with Congressional Leaders, 27 June 1950, Elsey Papers, Truman Presidential Library.

[30] Memorandum, Meeting with Congressional Leaders, 27 June 1950, Elsey Papers, Truman Presidential Library.

[31] Statement by the President, 27 June 1950, Elsey Papers, Truman Presidential Library. Also available in *Public Papers of the Presidents: Harry S. Truman, 1950,* 492.

[32] Donovan, *Tumultuous Years: The Presidency of Harry S. Truman, 1949–1953,* 209. See also Glen D. Paige, *The Korea Decision: June 24–30, 1950* (New York: Free Press, 1968), 193–200.

[33] McCullough, *Truman,* 781–82.

[34] Hess, *Presidential Decisions for War,* 26; Paige, *Korea Decision,* 216–61, 262–65; and Hamby, *Man of the People,* 538.

[35] Arthur V. Watkins, "War by Executive Order," *Western Political Quarterly* 4 (December 1951): 539–49.

[36] Fisher, "Korean War," 35. See also Charles A. Lofgren, "Mr. Truman's War: A Debate and Its Aftermath," *Review of Politics* 31 (April 1969): 223–41.

[37] For Truman's highest approval rating, see Fred I. Greenstein, *The Presidential Difference: Leadership Style from FDR to Clinton* (New York: Free Press, 2000; repr., Princeton: Princeton University Press, 2001), appendix. For Truman's approval rating upon leaving office, see Arthur M. Schlesinger Jr., "Rating the Presidents: Washington to Clinton," *Political Science Quarterly* 112 (Summer 1997): 188.

[38] Hamby, *Man of the People,* 539; Fisher, "The Korean War," 35–37; and McCullough, *Truman,* 782. See also "The President's News Conference of June 29, 1950," *Public Papers of the Presidents: Harry S. Truman, 1950,* 504.

[39] Hess, *Presidential Decisions for War,* 38; and Arthur M. Schlesinger Jr., *The Imperial Presidency* (New York: Popular Library, 1973). See also Fisher, "The Korean War," 36, for a discussion of Schlesinger's mea culpa on his earlier endorsement of Truman's actions.

[40] Truman, *Memoirs,* 2:369.

LESSONS FROM TRUMAN
Comparing the End of World War II and the End of the Cold War

General Brent Scowcroft

I am pleased and really honored to be part of this book on the thirty-third president. I am a great fan of President Harry Truman, although I am not a Truman scholar. Many scholars have studied and written about Truman, and this book includes papers on many aspects of his national security legacy and foreign policy. As other authors have pointed out, there are striking similarities as well as striking dissimilarities between the environment present at the end of World War II and that present at the end of the Cold War. I believe it is appropriate to look at those and compare the

*President Truman
with a favorite
slogan, July 1959.
(TPL, 60-20-1)*

problems that President Truman faced and the problems facing us now at the end of the Cold War era to see what we can learn.

One question discussed by many scholars, both in this book and over the fifty years since Truman's presidency, is about Truman as an individual and how was he able to achieve such extraordinary things, given his background as a common man from Independence, Missouri. Indeed, how was he able to do all that? I have an opinion about this question. As I have said many times, Truman was one of my national security heroes. He was *not* a foreign policy expert by any stretch of the imagination. But he was a student of history, which I think is one of the best groundings anyone can have in dealing with the problems of foreign relations and the presidency. And he embodied certain critical characteristics. First of all, he was comfortable with himself. He is reputed to have said that there are a million people who could do the job of president better than he, but that did not matter. He had the job and they did not. And that was the way Truman approached the presidency—no point in apologizing for anything or for who he was or who he was not. He was president and was going to do the job to the best of his ability. And he did.

He retained, for example, the difference or distinction between being himself and being the president. One of the things that impresses me about Truman was the reverence he always had for the office of the presidency. I wish all of our presidents had had this; some have not. And he had other essential qualities a president must have, foremost among them presidential leadership.

PRESIDENTIAL LEADERSHIP IN A NEW WORLD

There are two facets to presidential leadership that any successful president has to have. The first is the ability to make a decision and then stick with it after it has been made. Many presidential decisions are uncertain and difficult ones where, whatever he does, the president is going to be criticized by half the country. The result is often a tendency to hedge or to backpedal on a decision in an attempt to make everyone happy. In some areas, especially dealing with national security, such wavering can be devastating. Truman never made that mistake.

The second facet is the ability to choose good, strong people and to know when to listen to them and when not to listen to them. That is very important, but it is a difficult skill. Harry Truman was a master of all these practices. He was tough, even stubborn, and surrounded himself with strong, brilliant personnel: George Marshall, Dean Acheson, Dwight Eisenhower, Douglas MacArthur, all of whom were strong leaders in their own right. But, there was no doubt about who the true decision maker was, as some of these people found out in a painful way.

Truman came from a tradition in American foreign policy of not paying attention to foreign policy unless we were fighting a war. He took office at a time of dramatic transition from war to peace; but most importantly, he inherited the winding down of a war and the need to set a course for a future that he knew almost nothing about. President Roosevelt had not talked to Truman about international affairs and U.S. policy. Truman had only been vice president for a little less than three months when FDR died. Although he had had a couple of meetings with FDR, they had not dealt with these kinds of substantive issues. Truman did not know what was in the president's mind as to how this postwar world was to develop.

The Yalta Summit proved that the wartime allies were still together, although the strain was evident, and FDR still exuded confidence that he could handle "Uncle Joe Stalin." But Yalta also showed a pattern for the future that depended on the wartime allies managing the world together. Truman knew little more than that about the situation he was inheriting, so it was really one big blank slate he was facing. He found out about the atom bomb, for example, after his first meeting with Soviet Foreign Minister Molotov. Truman was still very new in office when Molotov came to see him in April 1945, and there was already a big argument about Poland. The Soviet Union was not sticking to the Yalta agreements on Poland. Molotov came in and made his pitch, following which President Truman apparently really "took him to the woodshed." Molotov reportedly told Truman that no one had ever talked to him that way before. Truman is said to have replied, "Well, if you carry out your agreements it won't happen again." After that meeting, Secretary of War Stimson said to the president, "We need to have a talk"—what they talked about was the atomic bomb. As head of the Truman Committee in the U.S. Senate, Truman knew that there was something being done about a bomb, but he did not know anything more than that—he did not know about the Manhattan Project and the atomic testing. So that was the kind of the framework—or, more properly, the lack of framework—in which Truman entered the presidency. It was really remarkable.

THE TRUMAN DOCTRINE AND THE SOVIET THREAT

As time passed, of course, the negative signs of Soviet behavior increased, and there was an increasing pattern of noncooperation and active hostility on the part of the Soviet Union. Early in 1946, Ambassador George Kennan sent his famous telegram, a prelude to his "Mr. X" essay, setting forth the policy of containment. The telegram laid out the difficulties facing the allies, described the pattern of Soviet behavior that had developed, and warned of what probably was going to come. Shortly after that, in March of 1946 in Fulton, Missouri, Winston Churchill made the famous "Iron Curtain" speech. This speech surprised many people—perhaps even President Truman himself—because Churchill said there was already an iron curtain, and we are now in a cold war. Yet events and policies were still in transition; Truman was caught between his advisors who were saying that the United States must respond strongly to these dangers in a new way and others (Henry Wallace and Eleanor Roosevelt, for instance) who were saying that Truman needed to follow FDR's policy of conciliation if we were going to get along with Stalin. They also urged the need to keep the wartime alliance.

As the negative signs increased, Truman decided on two paths to meet the emerging challenges. The first was to counter Soviet aggression designs through the Truman Doctrine. Greece and Turkey were actually imperiled by the Soviet Union; there was civil war in Greece, Turkey was being threatened, and the Soviets were refusing to evacuate Iran. So the Truman Doctrine was a clear reaction to threatened aggression. The most important impetus for the second path was the winter of 1946/47, which was a savage one in Europe. This caused slightly different concerns however, not about Soviet aggression, but that conditions might create a fertile field for communism in the heart of Europe. The response to this set of issues was the Marshall Plan.

These two responses were of the same general nature but dealt with different parts of the threat. In his inaugural address in 1949, Truman added a third part of the doctrine bearing his name, which became the groundwork or fundamental underpinnings of U.S. developmental aid programs. In these three initiatives, he outlined the whole concept of how to use economic assistance to not only contain the Soviet Union but also to reach out and stimulate world development. It is hard for us today, looking back, to see how farsighted this was.

The year 1947 also saw the construction of a national security apparatus in the United States. The country had operated ad hoc before Truman, throwing together some temporary structures for World War II; after the war, the United States found that the pre-war structure was hopelessly inadequate. Truman's response was the establishment of the Department of Defense, the Air Force, the National Security Council, and the Central Intelligence Agency. All the basic elements of the national security structure we have today were put in place by Harry Truman. The structure has evolved over time, but Truman created it.

In 1948, the militarization of the confrontation with the Soviets began with the Berlin blockade. President Truman's reaction to this was very wise and instructive. He did not go to extremes. He did not say we should *not* go to war over this, that it was just Berlin and we should thus acquiesce and make a deal. On the other hand, neither did he say we should mount up the tanks and crash through to Berlin. Instead he made a solid but careful decision to thwart the Soviet objectives without militarily confronting them at a time when we really were not prepared to confront them. And we were not ready—the United States had one division in Europe, and the future NATO countries together had roughly twelve divisions. The Soviets had eighty divisions. That was the balance. The Berlin blockade made it clear that we had to have an alliance of the Atlantic community to deal with a threat that was now being militarized.

Move forward to 1949, which was a bad year. The communists were victorious in China, and it became clear that the communists were on the march. At this time there was for us no real difference between the Russians and the Chinese. Then, in 1950, North Korea invaded South Korea. I agree with Truman's response, and George Elsey was right to see it as an unhesitating response. But, again, it was a moderate response focused on the issue at hand—not using atomic weapons, not taking the war to its source, which was either China or Russia at the time, but dealing with the issue at hand in a forceful but prudent way. This incident showed Truman's innovative use of the new (albeit partially stymied by the Soviets) United Nations, which established a pattern our country has used over and over again to involve the UN in military situations.

Looking back at those five years—one of the most remarkable periods in American history—the shifts that took place in foreign policy and national security policy and the mobilization of American interests in an entirely new direction were nothing short of amazing. Through it all, Truman enjoyed strong but very divided counsel. Truman listened to the advice, but when experts—even heroes like MacArthur—went too far in crossing him, they got fired. Truman had confidence not only in his own common sense, but in his ability to know in any situation whose counsel he should listen to. He never sought to escalate crises, but he pursued U.S. interests without hesitation and with a dogged determination. Truman was an institution builder: almost everywhere you look in the field of national security, you will find Harry Truman's hand. Truman gave us the structure of our national security institutions today—including the United Nations and peace enforcement—and the whole concept of foreign aid as a way not only to help countries deal with economic problems, but also to help the United States deal with many of our foreign policy issues.

THE END OF THE COLD WAR

Jumping ahead to the end of the Cold War, we see a period similar to the end of World War II, in that there was a sharp and decisive break in the pattern of international relations. Dramatic changes happened very, very suddenly. In that sense the two eras are similar, but there the similarities end, because in 1945 the developing Soviet threat framed the U.S. response, and it was a response to a very specific issue. Conversely, the absence of a threat at the end of the Cold War also framed our response, which was basically to drift for a decade or so. We went back to earlier patterns when foreign policy was an optional exercise. We were involved but saw no reason to develop a philosophy or strategy of foreign policy. There were no serious threats to U.S. security. The world was democratizing, and many believed that democracies don't fight democracies, and therefore we did not have to worry about international affairs any more. Accordingly, we paid little attention to world affairs and our role in them, even though some things were changing in a perilous way.

First of all, our nation did not realize what it really meant to be the only superpower. We had unparalleled power after World War II, but we were not the only superpower. The Soviet Union framed the responses that we made. As a result, when the Soviet Union disappeared, we really did not know how to behave. What should we do? What shouldn't we do? Sadly, we did not think that much about it. Neither did the rest of the world know how to behave toward us. There is always a natural resentment of the big guy on the block, and there was the reality that we were everywhere in the world; no other nation was spread so widely. So everything that happened tended to become our fault and, in addition, we were expected to have the solution to every problem that developed. In other words, we were considered both responsible for problems that developed and responsible for solving them.

A few other trends were developing. One was the rise of globalization, characterized by the growing porosity of national boundaries and inability of countries to control what came in and went out. Capital flows, environmental issues, and communications, especially television and movies—all these things were changing the face of the globe. But at the same time, there was a growth of intolerant nationalism, a desire for societies to break into ever smaller, more homogenous, and more intolerant political groupings. The former Yugoslavia is a good example of this. These were contradictory trends, but they were going on at the same time. When Harry Truman became president, the United Nations had 51 members. It now has 191, and most of those newer countries are poor, small, weak, and not very well able to care for their citizens in the manner we believe a state should. For the U.S., globalization is a generally positive force, leading to prosperity through the growing integration of countries. But for many of these 190 countries, globalization is the onslaught of a bewildering array of forces they cannot understand, let alone cope with. Globalization assaults their culture, their values, their families, their very identities in a way that is frightening. Furthermore, most of these forces have "United States" written all over them. Whether it is McDonald's, blue jeans, movies, or television, it is made in America. We have therefore become associated with forces that are destroying traditional life in much of the world, and I think this is the source of many problems we face today.

Another force is the rise of terrorism and its ability to cause great harm. Terrorism is no longer just a few machine guns or a homemade bomb, but organized, widespread, and very dangerous. Terrorists are impervious to most of the traditional pressures used in the military realm—deterrence, retaliation, and the like. So how can we cope with these forces? Terrorist strength was growing while we were not paying attention. The tragedy of 11 September 2001 was a wake-up call. Americans felt vulnerable, an emotional state that most of the world experiences frequently. Before that day, Americans' attitude was that wars do not happen in the United States, they happen overseas. The 9/11 attacks made us take stock of what had happened during the past decade, what the forces were, and what we ought to do about them. The result of this evaluation—partly by the public but especially within the administration—has been to come up with two different policy reactions.

Broadly speaking, these different strategic approaches may be called "traditional" and "transformational." The traditionalists—using many strategies established by Harry Truman—would reach out to our allies, reach out to international institutions, and try to deal cautiously and incrementally with the problems at hand. In contrast, the transformationalists' motto is to be bold. They see the world as needing reform and the United States as having the power to do it. They would act rapidly and not be tied down by tradition, by our allies, or by international organizations because the transformationalists know exactly what we have to do and see traditional approaches as slowing us down and weakening our resolve. Transformationalists would have us act quickly, and when we have acted, the rest of the world will realize we have done the right thing.

In this environment, unlike in the Truman period, it is not easy to discern what our guiding foreign policy principles should be. Looming over us are the 9/11 attacks and the threat of international terrorism, perhaps the biggest signpost since the Cold War. Traditional policy behavior got us successfully through the Cold War—no question about it. But has its time passed? Iraq may give us a clue as to the answer. How hard will it be to transform Iraq? How difficult a task is it to build a democracy? How transformationalist is it possible to be? What is the likely form of future conflict? A campaign against terrorism, for example, is a war not involving massed tanks, artillery, or aircraft; it is a war of intelligence, and to fight a war of intelligence, we have to have allies. It is not a matter of choice—we alone cannot gather the required intelligence on terrorists and their operations around the world, nor can we cut off terrorist finances by ourselves.

In the post–World War II world we faced one big threat and rose brilliantly to deal with that threat, but now there are a multitude of smaller problems and threats. The question is, how do we deal with them? No one threat is going to sink us, but could we find ourselves overwhelmed like Gulliver by the Lilliputians? Even a superpower can get overextended. At the present time, for example, roughly 40 percent of our ground combat power is overseas. Truman made extraordinarily wise choices for the United States in the face of grave peril. In the absence of the compelling force of peril, we have the opportunity, if we behave wisely, to produce a world far more prosperous and benevolent than anything Harry Truman could have imagined. But it will not happen by accident. We still have many choices ahead of us.

APPENDIX
Chronology of the Life of Harry S. Truman

1884   Harry S. Truman born in Lamar, Missouri (8 May).

1885   Truman family moved to a farm near Harrisonville, Missouri.

1887   Truman family moved to a farm near Grandview, Missouri.

1890   Truman family moved to Independence, Missouri.
Met Bess Wallace at First Presbyterian Church.

1892   Attended elementary school at Noland School in Independence.

1900   Served as page at Democratic National Convention in Kansas City.

1901   Graduated from Independence High School.
Attended Spalding Business College.

1902   Briefly employed in mailroom of *Kansas City Star*.

1902–3   Worked as timekeeper on Santa Fe Railroad construction.

1903   Truman family moved to Kansas City, Missouri.

1903–5   Employed as clerk with National Bank of Commerce in Kansas City.

1905–6   Bookkeeper with Union National Bank in Kansas City.

1905–11 Member, Battery B of Missouri National Guard.

1906   Returned to Grandview to help run family farm.

1910   Began to court Bess Wallace.

1911   Organized first Masonic Lodge in Grandview (Mason since 1909).

1914   Father died (2 November).
            Appointed as roads supervisor in Washington Township.

1915   Appointed as postmaster in Grandview.

1916   Established oil drilling company and served as treasurer (1916–19).

1917   Rejoined Missouri National Guard, Battery F, 2nd Missouri Artillery.
            Sworn into U.S. Army 129th Field Artillery unit as first lieutenant.

1918   Arrived in France (13 April).
            Promoted to captain (May), commanded Battery D, 129th Field Artillery unit, 35th Division.

1919   Discharged from war service (6 May).
            Married Bess Wallace at Trinity Episcopal Church (28 June).
            Moved to Independence home of mother-in-law, Madge Gates Wallace.
            Opened haberdashery store in Kansas City, Missouri.

1920   Appointed as major in Officers Reserve Corps.

1922   Elected as judge (county administrator) on Jackson County Court.

1923–25   Attended Kansas City School of Law.

1924   Defeated for reelection.
            Established Community Savings & Loan Association in Independence.

1926   Elected as judge of Jackson County Court (reelected in 1930).

1932   Promoted to colonel in U.S. Army Reserve.

1933   Appointed as federal reemployment director for Missouri.

1934 Elected to U.S. Senate (sworn in 3 January 1935).
Committees: Appropriations Committee (Military
 Subcommittee)
  Interstate Commerce Committee
  Public Buildings and Grounds Committee
  Committee on Printing

1940 Reelected to Senate.

1941 Proposed establishment of special Senate committee
 to investigate defense spending and contracts;
 chaired Senate Special Committee to Investigate the
 National Defense Program (Truman Committee).

1944 Spoke at ceremony launching USS *Missouri*.
Nominated as vice presidential candidate at
 Democratic National Convention (21 July).
Had first meeting with President Roosevelt (18
 August).
Elected vice president (7 November).

1945 Sworn in as vice president (20 January).
Became president on death of President Roosevelt
 (12 April).
Announced end of war in Europe (8 May).
Spoke at UN Charter Conference in San Francisco (26
 June).
Attended Potsdam Conference with Winston Churchill
 and Joseph Stalin
 (17 July to 2 August) to discuss future of Germany.
Announced dropping of first atomic bomb on
 Hiroshima (6 August).
Announced dropping of second atomic bomb on
 Nagasaki (9 August).
Announced end of war in Japan (14 August).
Presented 21-point program for reconversion from
 war and continuation
 of New Deal (6 September).

1946 Established Council of Economic Advisers (20
 February).
Arranged $3.75 billion loan to Great Britain.
Republicans won House and Senate in midterm
 elections (5 November).

Signed proclamation officially ending World War II (31 December).

1947   General George C. Marshall became new secretary of state.

Visited Mexico to continue FDR's Good Neighbor policy.

Requested $400 million for Greece and Turkey to fight spread of communism (Truman Doctrine) (12 March).

Peace treaties ratified with Italy, Hungary, Romania, Bulgaria.

National Security Act passed, establishing Central Intelligence Agency and National Security Commission.

Spoke at conference on peace and security in Rio de Janeiro; signed Inter-American Treaty of Reciprocal Assistance (Rio Pact).

1948   Passed Foreign Assistance Act providing for the European Recovery Program (Marshall Plan) (3 April).

Recognized State of Israel.

Signed Displaced Persons Act to admit thousands of Europeans to U.S.

Ordered Berlin airlift (26 June 1948 to 12 May 1949).

Received nomination for president at Democratic National Convention, but delegates from Alabama and Mississippi walked out in protest of Truman's support for civil rights (15 July).

Whistle-stop train campaign (6 September to 30 October).

Elected president (2 November).

1949   Dean Acheson became secretary of state.

Presidential inauguration (20 January).

Announced Point IV program to aid poor peoples of the world (20 January).

Signed National Security Act creating a unified Department of Defense.

Proclaimed North Atlantic Pact; NATO charged with implementation (24 August).

Announced successful Russian atomic test.

Signed Mutual Defense Assistance Act, providing for military assistance to North Atlantic Pact signatory nations (6 October).

1950   Ordered U.S. forces to aid South Koreans against communists from North Korea (26 June).

Ordered blockade of Korean coast (30 June); action supported by UN.

Requested supplemental funds from Congress for Korean effort.

Ordered government seizure of railroads to prevent strike.

Signed Defense Production Act, setting price, wage, and production amounts for Korean War.

General George Marshall became secretary of defense.

Met with General MacArthur, commander of Korean conflict, on Wake Island.

Assassination attempt by Puerto Rican nationalists (1 November).

Proclaimed national state of emergency after communist China enters the war in support of communist North Korea.

1951   Relieved General MacArthur of command for insubordination (11 April);
Lieutenant General Matthew Ridgway given command.

Supported emergency food relief to India.

Mutual Security Act passed, providing economic, military, technical aid to allies.

1952   Ordered government seizure of steel mills to prevent strikes; Supreme Court ruled the action unconstitutional a few days later.

Signed peace treaties with Japan, Australia, New Zealand, Philippines.

1953   Attended inauguration of Dwight D. Eisenhower; left office and returned home to Independence.

1955   Published *Memoirs: Year of Decisions*.
        Groundbreaking of Truman Presidential Library (8 May).

1956   Published *Memoirs: Years of Trial and Hope*.
        Toured Europe with Bess; met with Pope Pius XII and Winston Churchill; received honorary degree from Oxford University.
        Campaigned for Adlai Stevenson for president (even though Truman supported Averell Harriman).

1957   Began writing series of articles for newspapers around the country.
        Truman Presidential Library dedicated (6 July).

1958   National TV interview on CBS with Edward R. Murrow.
        Toured Europe with Bess for the second time.

1959   Truman birthplace in Lamar, Missouri, dedicated as state historic site (19 April).

1960   Published *Mr. Citizen*.
        Held press conference to endorse John F. Kennedy for president; campaigned for Kennedy.

1961   Participated in Kennedy inauguration.

1963   The Ahepa Truman Memorial was dedicated in Athens, Greece, in commemoration of the Truman Doctrine and in honor of former president Harry S. Truman.

1964   First of twenty-six half-hour TV shows (*Decisions: The Conflicts of Harry S. Truman*) aired in syndication.
        Received from the South Korean ambassador to the United States the "Order of Merit for the National Foundation Joongjang," the republic's highest honor.

1965   Addressed U.S. Senate; honored by them on his 80th birthday.
        Honored by President Lyndon Johnson during passage of Medicare Bill.

1966   Harry S. Truman Center for the Advancement of Peace
            ceremony in Jerusalem.

1968   President Johnson signed bill at Truman home
            designating UN Day (24 October).

1972   Harry Truman died at age 88 (26 December); interred
            in the Truman Presidential Library courtyard.

1982   Bess Truman died at age 97 (18 October); interred in
            the Truman Presidential Library courtyard.

Selected Bibliography

Containment

Deibel, Terry L., and John Lewis Gaddis. *Containment: Concept and Policy*. Washington DC: National Defense University, 1986.

Drew, S. Nelson, ed. *NSC-68: Forging the Strategy of Containment*. Washington DC: National Defense University, 1996.

Gaddis, John Lewis. "National Security: Strategies of Containment, Past and Future." *Hoover Digest* (Spring 2001): 116–24.

———. *Strategies of Containment: A Critical Appraisal of Postwar American National Security*. New York: Oxford University Press, 1982.

Litwak, Robert. *Rogue States and U.S. Foreign Policy: Containment After the Cold War*. Washington DC: Woodrow Wilson Center Press, 2000.

The Marshall Plan

Baun, Michael J. "The Marshall Plan: A Study of Morality and Foreign Policy." In *The Credibility of Institutions, Policies and Leadership: American Moral and Political Leadership in the Third World*, edited by Kenneth W. Thompson. Lanham, MD: University Press of America, 1985.

Clinton, David. "The Marshall Plan: A Non-Presidential Consensus?" In *Foreign Policy and Domestic Consensus: The Credibility of Institutions, Policies and Leadership*, edited by Richard A. Melanson and Kenneth W. Thompson. Lanham, MD: University Press of America, 1985.

Cronin, James E. "The Marshall Plan and Cold War Political Discourse." In *The Marshall Plan: Fifty Years Later*, edited by Martin A. Schain. New York: Palgrave, 2001.

Hogan, Michael J. *The Marshall Plan: America, Britain, and the Reconstruction of Western Europe, 1947–1952*. Cambridge: Cambridge University Press, 1987.

Mee, Charles L., Jr. *The Marshall Plan: The Launching of the Pax Americana*. New York: Simon & Schuster, 1984.

Menges, Constantine C., ed. *The Marshall Plan From Those Who Made It Succeed*. Lanham, MD: University Press of America, 1999.

Shapiro, Robert. "The Legacy of the Marshall Plan: American Public Support for Foreign Aid." In *The Marshall Plan: Fifty Years Later*, edited by Martin A. Schain. New York: Palgrave, 2001.

Wesler, Imanuel. "The Marshall Plan in Economic Perspective: Goals and Accomplishments." In *The Marshall Plan: Fifty Years Later,* edited by Martin A. Schain. New York: Palgrave, 2001.

NATO

Folly, Martin H. "Britain and the Issue of Italian Membership in NATO, 1948–1949." *Review of International Studies* 13 (1987): 177–96.

Furdson, Edward. *The European Defense Community: A History.* London: Macmillan, 1980.

Ismay, Lord. "Origins of the North Atlantic Treaty." In *NATO: The First Five Years, 1949–1954.* NATO Archives. [Paris?], [1954?].

Kaplan, Lawrence S. *A Community of Interests: NATO and the Military Assistance Program, 1948–1951.* Washington DC: Office of the Secretary of Defense, Historical Office, 1980.

Lansford, Tom. *All for One: Terrorism, NATO and the United States.* Aldershot, UK: Ashgate, 2002.

Osgood, Robert. *NATO: The Entangling Alliance.* Chicago: University of Chicago Press, 1962.

Smith, E. Timothy. "United States Security and the Integration of Italy into the Western Bloc, 1947–1949." In *NATO: The Founding of the Atlantic Alliance and the Integration of Europe,* edited by John R. Gillingham and Francis Heller. New York: St. Martin's, 1992.

Smith, Mark. *NATO Enlargement During the Cold War: Strategy and System in the Western Alliance.* New York: Palgrave, 2000.

Varsori, Antonio. "Great Britain and Italy, 1945–1956: The Partnership Between a Great Power and a Minor Power?" *Diplomacy and Statecraft* 3, no. 2 (1992): 188–228.

Walt, Stephen. *The Origins of Alliances.* Ithaca, NY: Cornell University Press, 1987.

Wiebes, Cees, and Bert Zeeman. "The Origins of Western Defense: Belgian and Dutch Perspectives, 1940–1949." In *The Atlantic Pact Forty Years Later: A Historical Reappraisal,* edited by Ehnio Di Nolfo. New York: Walter de Gruyter, 1991.

Wurm, Clemens, ed. *Western Europe and Germany: The Beginnings of European Integration, 1945–1960.* Oxford, UK: Berg, 1993.

The United Nations

Basic Facts About the United Nations. New York: United Nations, Department of Public Information, 1995.

Beichman, Arnold. *The "Other" State Department: The United States Mission to the United Nations—Its Role in the Making of Foreign Policy.* New York: Basic Books, 1967.

Brown, Benjamin H., and Joseph E. Johnson. *The U.S. and the U.N.* New York: Foreign Policy Association, 1954.

Eichelberger, Clark M. *U.N.: The First Ten Years.* New York: Harper & Brothers, 1955.

Mazuzan, George T. *Warren R. Austin at the U.N., 1946–1953*. Kent, OH: Kent State University Press, 1977.

Merrill, Dennis, ed., *Documentary History of the Truman Presidency*. Vol. 35, *The United Nations, 1945–1953: The Development of a World Organization*. Landham, MD: University Press of America, 2002.

United Nations. *Yearbook of the United Nations, 1950*. New York: United Nations, Department of Public Information, 1951.

The Korean War

Brune, Lester H. "Guns and Butter: The Pre–Korean War Dispute Over Budget Allocation." *American Journal of Economics and Sociology* 48 (July 1989): 357–71.

Fisher, Louis. "The Korean War: On What Legal Basis Did Truman Act?" *American Journal of International Law* 89 (January 1995): 21–39.

Heller, Francis H., ed. *The Korean War: A 25-year Perspective*. Lawrence: Regents Press of Kansas, 1977.

Hess, Gary R. *Presidential Decisions for War: Korea, Vietnam, and the Persian Gulf*. Baltimore: Johns Hopkins University Press, 2001.

Kaufman, Burton I. *The Korean War: Challenges in Crisis, Credibility, and Command*. New York: McGraw-Hill, 1997.

Lofgren, Charles A. "Mr. Truman's War: A Debate and Its Aftermath." *Review of Politics* 31 (April 1969): 223–41.

Paige, Glenn D. *The Korea Decision: June 24–30, 1950*. New York: Free Press, 1968.

The Cold War

Allison, Graham T. *Essence of Decision: Explaining the Cuban Missile Crisis*. Boston: Little, Brown, 1971.

Allison, Graham T., and Gregory F. Treverton, eds. *Rethinking America's Security: Beyond Cold War to a New World Order*. New York: W. W. Norton, 1992.

Gaddis, John Lewis. *We Now Know: Rethinking Cold War History*. New York: Oxford University Press, 1997.

Hammond, Paul Y. *The Cold War Years: American Foreign Policy Since 1945*. New York: Harcourt, Brace & World, 1969.

Lansford, Tom. *Evolution and Devolution: The Dynamics of Sovereignty in Post–Cold War Europe*. Aldershot, UK: Ashgate, 2000.

Leffler, Melvin P. *A Preponderance of Power: National Security, the Truman Administration, and the Cold War*. Stanford: Stanford University Press, 1992.

Lundestad, Geir. *America, Scandinavia and the Cold War, 1945–1949*. New York: Columbia University Press, 1980.

May, Ernest R., ed. *American Cold War Strategy: Interpreting NSC-68*. Boston: Bedford/St. Martin's, 1993.

Offner, Arnold A. *Another Such Victory: President Truman and the Cold War, 1945–1953*. Stanford: Stanford University Press, 2002.

———. "Another Such Victory: President Truman, American Foreign Policy and the Cold War." *Diplomatic History* 23 (Spring 1999): 131–32.

Reynolds, David. "The European Dimension of the Cold War." In *Origins of the Cold War: An International History,* edited by Melvyn Leffler and David S. Painter. London: Routledge, 1994.

Ruggie, John Gerard. "Third Try at World Order? America and Multilateralism After the Cold War." *Political Science Quarterly* 109 (Fall 1994): 553–70.

Schweizer, Peter. *Victory: The Reagan Administration's Secret Strategy that Hastened the Collapse of the Soviet Union.* New York: Atlantic Monthly Press, 1994.

Yergin, Daniel. *Shattered Peace: The Origins of the Cold War and the National Security State.* Boston: Little, Brown, 1977.

National Security

Daalder, Ivo H., and James M. Lindsay. "The Bush Revolution: The Remaking of America's Foreign Policy." In *The George W. Bush Presidency: An Early Assessment,* edited by Fred I. Greenstein. Baltimore: Johns Hopkins University Press, 2004.

Downs, George W., and Keisuke Iida. "Assessing the Theoretical Case Against Collective Security." In *Collective Security Beyond the Cold War,* edited by George W. Downs. Ann Arbor: University of Michigan Press, 1994.

Gilpin, Robert. *War and Change in World Politics.* New York: Cambridge University Press, 1981.

Hogan, Michael J. *A Cross of Iron: Harry S. Truman and the Origins of the National Security State, 1945–1954.* Cambridge: Cambridge University Press, 1998.

Hook, Steven W., and John Spanier. *American Foreign Policy Since World War II.* 15th ed. Washington DC: Congressional Quarterly Press, 2000.

Kegley, Charles, Eugene R. Wittkopf, and James Scott. *American Foreign Policy,* 6th ed. Belmont, CA: Wadsworth, 2003.

Kennan, George F. *American Diplomacy, 1900–1950.* Chicago: University of Chicago Press, 1951.

——— [Mr. X, pseud.]. "The Sources of Soviet Conduct." *Foreign Affairs* (July 1947): 575–76. Reprint, *Foreign Affairs* 65 (Spring 1987): 852–68.

McCormick, James. *American Foreign Policy and Process,* 3rd ed. Itasca, IL: F. E. Peacock, 1998.

Rock, Stephen R. *Why Peace Breaks Out: Great Power Rapprochement in Historical Perspective.* Chapel Hill: University of North Carolina Press, 1989.

Smith, Gaddis. *The Last Years of the Monroe Doctrine.* New York: Hill & Wang, 1994.

———. *American Secretaries of State and Their Diplomacy: Dean Acheson.* New York: Cooper Square, 1972.

Smith, Tony. *America's Mission: The United States and the Worldwide Struggle for Democracy in the Twentieth Century.* Princeton: Princeton University Press, 1994.

Van Dyke, Vernon, and Edward Lane Lewis. "Senator Taft and American Security." *Journal of Politics* 14 (May 1952): 177–202.

Williams, Andrew. *Failed Imaginations: New World Orders of the Twentieth Century.* New York: Manchester University Press, 1998.

Truman (Biographies)

Donovan, Robert J. *Conflict and Crisis: The Presidency of Harry S. Truman, 1945–1948.* New York: W. W. Norton, 1977.

———. *Tumultuous Years: The Presidency of Harry S. Truman, 1949–1953.* New York: W. W. Norton, 1982.

Ferrell, Robert H. *Harry S. Truman and the Modern Presidency.* Boston: Little, Brown, 1983.

———, ed. *Dear Bess: The Letters from Harry to Bess Truman, 1910–1959.* New York: Harper & Row, 1983.

———, ed. *Off the Record: The Private Papers of Harry S. Truman.* New York: Harper & Row, 1980.

Gardner, Michael R. *Harry Truman and Civil Rights: Moral Courage and Political Risks.* Carbondale: Southern Illinois University Press, 2002.

Hamby, Alonzo L. *Man of the People: A Life of Harry S. Truman.* New York: Oxford University Press, 1995.

Haynes, Richard F. *The Awesome Power: Harry S. Truman as Commander in Chief.* Baton Rouge: Louisiana State University Press, 1973.

Hechler, Ken. *Working with Truman.* New York: Putnam, 1982.

Heller, Francis H., ed. *Economics and the Truman Administration.* Lawrence: Regents Press of Kansas, 1981.

Jenkins, Roy. *Truman.* New York: Harper & Row, 1986.

McCullough, David. *Truman.* New York: Simon & Schuster, 1992.

Miller, Merle. *Plain Speaking: An Oral Biography of Harry S. Truman.* New York: Greenwich House, 1985.

Miller, Richard Lawrence. *Truman: The Rise to Power.* New York: McGraw-Hill, 1986.

Thompson, Kenneth W., ed. *Portraits of American Presidents.* Vol. 2, *The Truman Presidency: Intimate Perspectives.* Lanham, MD: University Press of America, 1984.

Truman, Harry S. *Mr. Citizen.* New York: Bernard Geis, 1960.

———. *Memoirs.* Vol. 1: *Year of Decisions.* Garden City, NY: Doubleday, 1955.

———. *Memoirs.* Vol. 2: *Years of Trials and Hope.* Garden City, NY: Doubleday, 1956.

————. *Public Papers of the Presidents, Harry S. Truman, Containing the Public Messages, Speeches and Statements of the President. 1945–1953*. 8 vols. Washington DC: Government Printing Office, 1961–66.

Truman, Margaret. *Bess W. Truman*. New York: Macmillan, 1986.

————. *Harry S. Truman*. New York: William Morrow, 1973.

The Presidency (General Works)

Greenstein, Fred I. *The Presidential Difference: Leadership Style from FDR to Clinton*. New York: Free Press, 2000. Reprint, Princeton: Princeton University Press, 2001.

————. *The George W. Bush Presidency: An Early Assessment*. Baltimore: Johns Hopkins University Press, 2004.

Haass, Richard. "Squandered Presidency: Demanding More from the Commander in Chief." *Foreign Affairs* (May/June 2000): 136–40.

Neustadt, Richard. *Presidential Power and the Modern Presidents: The Politics of Leadership from Roosevelt to Reagan*. New York: Free Press, 1990.

Oye, Kenneth A., Robert J. Lieber, and Donald Rothchild, eds. *Eagle Resurgent? The Reagan Era in American Foreign Policy*. Boston: Little, Brown, 1987.

Schlesinger, Arthur M., Jr. *The Imperial Presidency*. New York: Popular Library, 1973.

————. "Rating the Presidents: Washington to Clinton," *Political Science Quarterly* 112 (Summer 1997): 179–90.

Watkins, Arthur V. "War by Executive Order." *Western Political Quarterly* 4 (December 1951): 539–49.

Miscellaneous Sources and Memoirs

Acheson, Dean. *Present at the Creation: My Years in the State Department*. New York: W. W. Norton, 1969.

Adenauer, Konrad. *Memoirs, 1945–1966*. Chicago: Henry Regnery, 1966.

Campbell, Thomas M., and George C. Herring, eds. *The Diaries of Edward R. Stettinius Jr., 1943–1946*. New York: New Viewpoints, 1975.

Carpenter, Francis W. *Men in Glass Houses*. New York: McBride, 1951.

Jessup, Philip C. *The Birth of Nations*. New York: Columbia University Press, 1974.

Jewell, Malcolm E. "The Senate Republican Policy Committee and Foreign Policy." *Western Political Quarterly* 12 (December 1959): 966–80.

Kennan, George F. *Memoirs*. Boston: Little, Brown, 1967.

MacArthur, Douglas. *Reminiscences*. New York: McGraw-Hill, 1964.

Matthews, Geoffrey. "Robert A. Taft, the Constitution and American Foreign Policy, 1939–1953." *Journal of Contemporary History* 17 (July 1982): 507–22.

Montgomery, Bernard Law. *The Memoirs of Field Marshall Montgomery.* New York: World Publishing, 1958.

Rigdon, William. *The White House Sailor.* Garden City, NY: Doubleday, 1962.

CONTRIBUTORS

MEENA BOSE received her PhD from Princeton University and received the "Best Dissertation on the Presidency" award from the Center for Presidential Studies. She is associate professor of political science at the U.S. Military Academy at West Point. Bose is an expert on presidential politics and U.S. foreign policy. She is the author of numerous articles and of the book *Shaping and Signaling Presidential Policy: The National Security Decision Making of Eisenhower and Kennedy,* and is editor of *From Cold War to New World Order: The Foreign Policy of George H. W. Bush.*

DOUGLAS M. BRATTEBO received his PhD from the University of Maryland at College Park and his J.D. from Georgetown University Law Center. He is assistant professor of political science at the U.S. Naval Academy. He is also a member of the Maryland bar. In May 2002, he won the Naval Academy's campus-wide Apgar Award for Teaching Excellence. Brattebo is the author of numerous articles and book chapters, guest editor of "The Presidency, the Navy, and the War on Terror" (a special issue of *White House Studies,* 2004), and is the editor of a forthcoming book on the same topic.

FRANK T. BROGAN is the president of Florida Atlantic University. An honors graduate from the University of Cincinnati, Brogan earned his master's degree from Florida Atlantic University. After a successful career as a teacher and school principal, Brogan was elected superintendent of schools for Martin County, Florida and later was elected Florida's commissioner of education. Brogan ran successfully for lieutenant governor of Florida, served with Governor Jeb Bush, and was reelected to a second term. Brogan has received numerous awards recognizing his community and public service and serves on the boards of several community and educational organizations in Florida.

CLIFTON TRUMAN DANIEL is the grandson of Harry and Bess Truman and the son of the President's only child, Margaret. Daniel serves as the director of public relations for Truman College in Chicago.

JOHN DAVIS completed his PhD at Howard University. He teaches courses on U.S. foreign policy, international relations, and national security at Howard University in Washington DC and is the author of numerous articles and book chapters. Davis worked previously for the National Defense University at Fort McNair in the nation's capital, conducting research on national security issues.

MICHAEL J. DEVINE completed his PhD at Ohio State University. He is director of the Truman Presidential Museum and Library and president of the Harry S. Truman Library Institute. A respected scholar and diplomatic historian with several publications to his credit, Devine served as a senior Fulbright lecturer in Korea and a distinguished professor in China. Devine was formerly the Illinois state historian and director of the American Heritage Museum at the University of Wyoming.

GEORGE M. ELSEY served as an aide to President Franklin D. Roosevelt during World War II. As an aide in the White House of President Harry Truman, he played a key role in developing the Truman Doctrine, Truman's civil rights messages to Congress, the Executive Orders to end segregation in the armed forces, and the famous whistle-stop train speeches during the 1948 campaign. An honors graduate from Princeton University with a master's degree from Harvard University, Elsey also served as a naval intelligence officer during World War II, was at Omaha Beach on D-Day in 1944, and was discharged with the rank of commander. Elsey has served on the boards of numerous corporations, the Brookings Institution, National Geographic, the George C. Marshall Foundation, on the Advisory Committee on the Presidential Libraries, and as president of the White House Historical Association and vice chairman of the National Trust for Historic Preservation. Elsey is also well known for his involvement in the American Red Cross, beginning in 1953 and culminating in his tenure as the organization's president from 1970 to 1983 and as an official with the International Federation of Red Cross from 1973 to 1987. He is the recipient of countless distinguished awards and honors, including being named to the Order of the British Empire by King George VI and the Order of St. John by Queen Elizabeth II.

KEN HECHLER served in the White House of President Harry Truman as research director, speechwriter, and special assistant to the president. After his service in the Truman administration, Hechler was elected to nine terms in Congress (1957–77) as representative from West Virginia, and was elected to four four-year terms as West Virginia's secretary of state (1985–2001). A graduate of Swarthmore College, Hechler received his PhD from Columbia University and later taught political science at Columbia University, Barnard College, Princeton University, and Marshall University. Hechler also worked with Judge Samuel I. Rosenman and President Franklin D. Roosevelt in editing the thirteen-volume *Public Papers and Addresses of Franklin D. Roosevelt,* served as a combat historian in the European theater of operations in World War II, and has written six books, including *The Bridge at Remagen,* which sold 600,000 copies and was made into a motion picture.

MILTON KAYLE served in the White House as special assistant to President Harry Truman. A graduate of Hamilton College and Harvard Law School, Kayle served as a sergeant in the U.S. Infantry in the European theater of World War II and later worked in the Bureau of Budget and the Office of Defense Mobilization. After the Truman presidency, Kayle went on to establish a distinguished career in New York City as a specialist in the field of intellectual property. Kayle continues his involvement with Truman by serving on the board of directors and as secretary of the Truman Library Institute and also functioned as the Institute's representative on the Advisory Committee on the Presidential Libraries.

TOM LANSFORD completed his PhD at Old Dominion University. He is assistant professor of political science at the University of Southern Mississippi and a fellow of the Frank Maria Center for International Politics and Ethics. Lansford is a member of the governing board of the National Social Science Association, associate editor of the journal *White House Studies,* and book review editor for the *International Journal of Politics and Ethics.* He has published articles in numerous journals and is the author of a number of books, most recently *The Lords of Foggy Bottom: The American Secretaries of State and the World They Shaped; Evolution and Devolution: The Dynamics of Sovereignty and Security in Post–Cold War Europe;* and *All for One: Terrorism, NATO, and the United States.*

GENERAL BRENT SCOWCROFT is a graduate of the U.S. Military Academy at West Point and earned his PhD from Columbia University. Scowcroft is retired from the U.S. Air Force after a long and very distinguished career that began with a commission in the Army Air Forces and included senior positions in the Joint Chiefs of Staff, the headquarters of the Air Force, assistant attache in the American embassy in Belgrade, and a faculty position at West Point. He served as President Richard Nixon's military assistant and deputy national security advisor and later as national security advisor to President Gerald Ford and President George H. W. Bush. Scowcroft has chaired or served on the boards of many organizations, including several presidential committees and blue-ribbon commissions on such issues as arms control, defense management, and the Iran-contra investigation. The general has chaired President George W. Bush's Foreign Intelligence Advisory Board and sits on the boards of the Gerald R. Ford Foundation, the George C. Marshall Foundation, the Center for Strategic and International Studies, the Atlantic Council, the Bush Presidential Library, and many other organizations. Scowcroft is the president of the Forum for International Policy and the Scowcroft Group, both in Washington DC. The recipient of many military decorations and awards, Scowcroft received the Presidential Medal of Freedom and was made an Honorary Knight of the British Empire by Her Majesty Queen Elizabeth II.

ROBERT P. WATSON received his PhD from Florida Atlantic University. He is associate professor of political science at Florida Atlantic University and founding editor of the journal *White House Studies.* The author or editor of twenty-five books, Watson has published over a hundred articles and chapters on such topics as the presidency, first ladies, campaigns/elections, civil rights, environmental policy, bureaucracy, and American politics. Watson has been interviewed by CNN, MSNBC, *USA Today,* and numerous other media outlets, appeared on C-SPAN's *Book TV* program, was a guest for CNN.com's coverage of the 2001 presidential inauguration, and directed the first-ever *Report to the First Lady,* which was presented to the White House in 2001. He serves on the boards on several journals, academic associations, and presidential foundations—including the Key West Harry S. Truman Foundation—and has lectured as a visiting scholar at many universities and presidential sites, including the Truman Presidential Museum and Library.

ROBERT J. WOLZ is executive director of the Harry S. Truman Little White House, a position he has held since 1999. He has extensive experience with historic sites and history tourism, and has organized historical exhibits on such topics as Florida history, Native American history, and the Grand Army of the Republic. He is the author of *The Legacy of the Harry S. Truman Little White House: Presidents in Paradise, Collecting the Grand Army of the Republic and its Allied Orders,* and several articles on Florida history. Wolz is past vice commander-in-chief and national historian of the Sons of Union Veterans of the Civil War and a graduate of Youngstown State University with a degree in American history.

INDEX

Headnote: Photographs are identified by **bold** page numbers.